THE ANTERIOR CONSTRUCTION
IN CLASSICAL HEBREW

THE SOCIETY OF BIBLICAL LITERATURE
MONOGRAPH SERIES

Editor
Terence E. Fretheim

Number 50
THE ANTERIOR CONSTRUCTION
IN CLASSICAL HEBREW

by
Ziony Zevit

Ziony Zevit

THE ANTERIOR CONSTRUCTION IN CLASSICAL HEBREW

Society of Biblical Literature
Monograph Series

Scholars Press
Atlanta, Georgia

THE ANTERIOR CONSTRUCTION IN CLASSICAL HEBREW

by
Ziony Zevit

Library of Congress Cataloging in Publication Data
Zevit, Ziony.
    The anterior construction in classical Hebrew / Ziony Zevit.
       p.   cm. — (Society of Biblical Literature monograph series ;
   no. 50)
    Includes bibliographical references and indexes.
    ISBN 0-7885-0443-6 (alk. paper); 0-7885-0625-0 (paper : alk. paper).
    1. Hebrew language—Tense. 2. Bible. O.T.—Language, style.
   3. Narration in the Bible. I. Title. II. Series.
PJ4659.Z48   1998
492.4'5—dc21   98-6045
                              CIP

08 07 06 05 04 03 02 01 00   5 4 3

Printed in the United States of America
on acid-free paper

CONTENTS

בן שמונים לגבורות (אבות ה כא)

for my parents

David and Zola Zevit

in their decade of special strength
for their love, wisdom, and encouragement

ACKNOWLEDGMENTS

It is my pleasure to express sincere thanks to those whose expertise, insights, and comments have contributed to the development of this study, though not always in the way that they anticipated.

I thank Anson F. Rainey for his response to a presentation that I made at the annual Society of Biblical Literature meeting in 1987—indirectly, he got the whole ball rolling—and Stephen A. Kaufman for some sharp questions to a paper presented at the annual American Oriental Society meeting in 1996. I learned much about the literary application of the construction from discussions with a host of individuals who attended my presentation to the Faculty Seminar of the Department of Hebrew Language at Bar Ilan University in 1995, particularly from Maya Fruchtman and Menahem Z. Kaddari. My colleague at the University of Judaism, Eliezer Slomovic, never failed to direct me to informative examples and informing passages. Terence E. Fretheim, editor of the monograph series, and two anonymous readers provided much useful criticism of an earlier version of this study and made helpful suggestions that greatly influenced my discussion of aspect and mood. Daryl Jefferies prepared the manuscript for publication.

To all, *tōdāh*.

PREFACE

Exegesis is about presentation and interpretation, *what* a narrative says and means. Sometimes, but not always, the expositor deals also with the questions of *how* a texts means and *why*. The *how* questions concern matters of lexicon, literary convention, as well as literary, cultural, and pragmatic contexts. *Why* questions concern lexicon, semantics, and grammar.

Analytically, a critical reader is aware of the differences between the *whats*, *whys*, and *hows* of meaning. Practically, however, the *whys*, and even the *hows* are submerged during most reading, taken for granted as the known, conventional stuff of communications in written narrative. Attention is focused on the communication, not on the vehicle. A reader engages the narrative like a playgoer the characters acted on a stage. Should a character flub a line, jarring a playgoer's suspension of disbelief, the actor becomes obvious, the trickery of language uncovered, and art exposed as artifice. Similarly, most readers become aware of language as vehicle in a narrative only when it fails as a vehicle, a word is misspelled, a grammatical infelicity occurs. Then, a reader's attention switches from message to medium, from content to construction. The demasking occurs only, of course, when the playgoer or reader is capable. Individuals lacking linguistic subtlety miss the errors as well as the creative fine points of the composition.

The first objective of this study is to clarify a grammatical matter of the *why* category that is recognized but imperfectly by contemporary students of biblical Hebrew and Semitic linguistics. Inadequately known, it has not been incorporated into the bundle of grammatical parsing information with which linguistically competent readers regularly discern meaning in texts. As a consequence, because contemporary readers fail to respond to linguistic information embedded deeply in the text, they miss some compositional fine points. This affects the interpretation of many biblical passages and the appreciation of aesthetic subtleties in the ancient compositions.

The particular grammatical matter involved, labeled here the "anterior construction," bears significant implications for reconsidering the semantics of classical Hebrew's verbal system—a matter relevant to the concerns of both Semitists and biblical expositors. The second objective of this study is to explore these implications and to provide a model that reconceives what types of information are provided by the verbal system and that explains what parts of the system provide the different types of information.

ABBREVIATIONS

AI	Arad Inscription
ASOR	American Schools of Oriental Research
BO	*Bibliotheca orientalis*
CIS	Corpus inscriptionum semiticarum
ErIsr	Eretz Israel
HAR	Hebrew Annual Review
HS	*Hebrew Studies*
HSM	Harvard Semitic Monographs
HUCA	*Hebrew Union College Annual*
IEJ	*Israel Exploration Journal*
IOS	*Israel Oriental Society*
JANESCU	*Journal of the Ancient Near Eastern Society of Columbia University*
JBL	*Journal of Biblical Literature*
JNSL	*Journal of Northwest Semitic Languages*
JQR	*Jewish Quarterly Review*
JSOTSup	Journal for the Study of the Old Testament—Supplement Series
JSS	*Journal of Semitic Studies*
KAI	H. Donner and W. Rollig, *Kanaanäische und aramäische Inschriften*
KTU	*Keilalphabetischen Texte aus Ugarit*
Leš	*Lešonénu*
Or	*Orientalia* (Rome)
ScrHier	Scripta hierosolymitana
SSN	Studia semitica neerlandica
UF	*Ugarit-Forschungen*
VT	*Vetus Testamentum*
ZAH	*Zeitschrift für Althebraistik*

I

THE CHARACTERISTIC STYLE OF HEBREW NARRATIVE

Most biblical prose consists of narratives about past events that involve slightly different styles and reflect various degrees of artistry.[1] No matter the style or the particular creative ploy employed by any author, the syntax of all such prose is characterized by syndetic constructions: words, phrases, clauses, and sentences of various types coordinated by the conjunctive *waw*, "and." Clauses connected this way may be either paratactic, i.e., coordinate, or hypotactic, i.e., subordinate, but parataxis predominates.[2] This characteristic, represented fairly in the *King James Version* of 1611, and all but eliminated in modern translations, may cause contemporary readers to view biblical prose as lengthy strings of run-on compound and compound-complex sentences.[3]

Driven by the *waw* consecutive construction, a conditioned allomorph of *waw* conjunctive, narratives proceed rapidly from scene to coordinated scene,

---

[1] J. Licht, *Storytelling in the Bible* (Jerusalem: Magnes, 1978) 29–33; A. Berlin, *Poetics and Interpretation of Biblical Narrative* (Sheffield: Almond Press, 1983) 43–59; M. Sternberg, *The Poetics of Biblical Narrative. Ideological Literature and the Drama of Reading* (Bloomington, IN: Indiana University Press, 1985) 58–128.

[2] J. Blau, *A Grammar of Biblical Hebrew* (Wiesbaden: O. Harrasowitz, 1976) 106, §105. A. Niccacci notes that due to contemporary conventions in European languages, clauses are often represented as subordinate even when they are not (*The Syntax of the Verb in Classical Hebrew Prose* [JSOTSup 86; Sheffield: JSOT Press, 1990] 128, §95).

T. A. van Dijk's essay, "Connectives in Text Grammar and Text Logic," provides theoretical models and terminology that may help clarify what is usually described loosely as "the syntax" of *waw* (*Grammars and Descriptions (Studies in Text Theory and Text Analysis)* [eds. T. A. van Dijk and J. S. Petöfi; Berlin: W. de Gruyter, 1977] 11–63).

[3] R. Alter departs from this contemporary practice, conscientiously rendering them in his translation and commentary (*Genesis* [New York: W. W. Norton & Co., 1996]). Proper punctuation eliminates the run-on effect.

paced more like an American than a European film.[4] The movie analogy, however, is not completely adequate because biblical narratives are usually deficient in descriptions of visual phenomena relative to setting and characters (and because they do not refer usually to the psychological states of characters that could be expressed either through body language or tone of voice). The narratives are, however, rich in dialogues and brief descriptions of kinetic activities that advance action.[5] Therefore, a second analogy complements the first. Biblical narratives are also like radio dramas in which dialogues comprise the scene and a narrator describes actions that segue from scene to scene.

Authors working within the conventions of Israelite *belles lettres* employed such descriptions to advance scenes and reported dialogues to develop plot and to imply the nature and motivations of the various characters. More laconic than loquacious, theirs was a literature of understatement and nuance, characteristically anecdotic rather than epic. This is generally the case even in the extended story cycles of Abraham, Jacob, Moses, Joshua, Gideon, Jephtha, Samson, and Saul.

The Joseph, David-Solomon, and Esther narrative complexes, with their more epic cast, are different. These feature recurring characters, allusions to earlier reported events, and the resolution of issues reported in early scenes near the end of the complex. For example, the looming threat of revenge for

---

[4] Blau, *A Grammar*, 46, §20.3; E. Qimron, "Consecutive and Conjunctive Imperfect: The Form of the Imperfect with Waw in Biblical Hebrew," *JQR* 77 (1987) 150–51; M. S. Smith, *The Origins and Development of the Waw Consecutive* (Atlanta: Scholars Press, 1991) 14–15, 27. J. C. L. Gibson describes the range of clauses coordinated by *waw* in classical Hebrew ("Coordination by Vav in Biblical Hebrew," *Words Remembered, Texts Renewed. Essays in Honor of John F. A. Sawyer* (eds. J. Davies et al.; JSOTSup 195; Sheffield: Sheffield Academic Press, 1995] 272–79).

D. L. Washburn hypothesizes that the *wa* + doubling element is not a syntactic marker connecting what comes after it with what comes before, but an inflectional morpheme signaling a separate thought ("Chomsky's Separation of Syntax and Semantics," *HS* 35 [1994] 27). He postulates that this *waw* is distinct from the conjunctive *waw*, a proposition contradicted by its non-appearance in poetic contexts as well as by the appearance of the conjunctive *waw* in identical contexts in other Northwest Semitic dialects. Furthermore, the postulate neither clarifies nor enhances understanding of the element in Hebrew itself.

[5] The best concise treatment of how biblical narrative presented "reality" remains that of E. Auerbach, *Mimesis: The Representation of Reality in Western Literature* (Princeton: Princeton University Press, 1953) 3–23. Auerbach's characterization of ancient Hebrew narrative in contrast with the Greek epic tradition of Homer is valid also for other ancient Near Eastern epic traditions such as those in Ugaritic and Akkadian.

the kidnapping of Joseph in Genesis 37, a leitmotif in chapters 42–43, is resolved only in Genesis 50 where all is forgiven. Similarly, David's tactical decisions not to exact retribution from former enemies, opponents, and even dangerous allies in 2 Sam 3:26–39; 16:9–14; and 19:16–23 are revealed as part of a strategy in 1 Kgs 2:1–9 that is executed in 1 Kgs 2:28–33, 36–46. These expansive narratives, however, are notable exceptions. Pregnant pericopes, either in isolation or sparse concatenation, are featured more often.

Ancient audiences, i.e., hearers—and even until the pre-modern period readers heard these narratives since texts were generally read aloud[6]— interpreted texts within these same conventions. Their life experience and geographical preknowledge combined with imag(e)-ination suggested mental images of a character's physical appearance as well as of the settings in which a character acted. Melded with an audience's own cultural norms, life experiences, and sophistication, these enabled Iron Age Israelites to intuit the motives behind characters' actions.[7]

Authors of these quick-paced, compact narratives were confronted by the problem of how to describe a) episodes concurrent with the main line narrative or b) background events out of sequence with the main narrative. One particular problem associated with background was how to provide information relevant to an upcoming segment of narrative about events that had transpired prior to the point in the past at which the main narrative line stood, but which had not been mentioned heretofore. In other words, the author's problem was how to express that an event had taken place prior to the event in the past that they had just described, i.e., how to indicate the past to the past.

Although translations into European languages regularly render Hebrew verbs in various contexts as pluperfects and although grammars do indicate that certain Hebrew verb forms sometimes express this meaning, Hebrew lacks a conjugated verbal form marking this chronological sequencing of events.

---

[6] This statement reflects the consensus among historians. Silent reading in antiquity was known, but in rather restricted settings. Cf. F. D. Gilliard, "More Silent Reading in Antiquity. *Non Omne Verbum Sonabat*," *JBL* 112 (1993) 689–94.

[7] This type of narrative tradition partially explains the great license taken in representational art, from the mosaic floors of Palestinian synagogues and the walls of the synagogue in Dura Europas to the works of the European masters, that represent imaginatively all that which biblical narratives left undescribed. It also clarifies the great variety of literary readings produced by contemporary interpreters in a post-Freudian, post-Jungian, post-Adlerian world as well as the license taken by those who created the homiletic midrashim.

The first objective of this study is to describe a device in biblical Hebrew, the anterior construction, that marks this chronological sequencing of events, its functions in narrative, and how it affects the meaning and interpretation of narrative—its exegetical pay-off. The second objective is to consider the implications of this device for comprehending the marking of time by the Hebrew verbal system and how it evolved within that system.

The study thus has two foci: one, a feature of classical Hebrew narratology; the other, indications of time in the Hebrew verbal system. Even though each focus must be analyzed separately, the two are interrelated. Although the second focus operates at a primal, deep structural level of the language, it is only observed on the higher surface level where meaning is communicated in a comprehensible context. Therefore, both foci must be considered in tandem.

Chapter II builds on the characterization of narrative presented above, but concentrates on a few specific points. It describes a) how Western exegetic tradition in the medieval period came to recognize the occasional chronological reversal in an advancing story line and b) how, during the nineteenth and twentieth centuries, some of these reversals came to be considered as implicit in the morphology of verbs. It indicates how this interpretative move was a consequence of descriptions of Hebrew that assumed the universal applicability of European grammatical constructs. Expanding on contemporary critiques of this view, the chapter demonstrates why descriptions of Hebrew based on it actually misinterpret significant elements of Hebrew grammar.

Chapter III continues the grammatical discussion of chapter II. It presents the "Anterior Construction," a syntactic construction used to indicate the past to the past in Hebrew, Moabite, and Phoenician narrative. This chapter a) discusses selected passages from which the construction was induced, b) indicates how recognizing the construction clarifies information and enhances understanding, and c) lists over 100 relevant examples.

Chapter IV evaluates briefly the role of the anterior construction as a backgrounding device in Hebrew narratology and compares it to other types of backgrounding. The chapter also distinguishes between common anticipatory backgrounding and the rarer postponed or retrospective backgrounding expressed through the anterior construction.

Chapter V resumes the conclusions of chapter III in the light of chapter IV. It discusses the major implication of the anterior construction for comprehending the Hebrew verbal system. Chapter V challenges the widely held notion that the system indicates aspect rather than tense and postulates that from the perspective of advances in general linguistics and the study of linguistic typology, Hebrew should be described as tensed.

Chapter VI submits that the two Hebrew tenses described in chapter V are indicated through four distinct forms, two *yiqtols* and two *qatals*, and that these were distinguished phonemically. The argument is supported by data from Moabite, Aramaic, and Phoenician, as well as by data from the masoretic tone system. This chapter also provides a brief sketch of how tense, aspect, and mood were expressed through the linguistic resources of the language.

Chapter VII resumes discussion of the narratological conclusions of chapters III and IV, suggesting in light of chapters V and VI how the anterior construction may have emerged in Hebrew and other cognate languages.

II

EXEGETIC INTIMATIONS
AND THE MORPHOLOGIC SOLUTION

The great medieval exegete, Rashi, R̲abbi S̲helomo ben I̲saac (1040–1105 CE), pointed to a handful of passages where he intuited from the inner logic of the narrative that some events were mentioned out of chronological sequence:

> Gen 4:1, *wh'dm yd'*, and the man knew—*kbr qwdm h'nyn šl m'lh*, already before the aforementioned matter (and therefore should be understood "and the man had known"—zz).[1]

Since Rashi did not provide reasons for his observations, they have to be inferred from his method of close reading. His comment on Gen 4:1 may have been stimulated by Gen 3:15a which seems to presuppose that the "seed" of both the serpent and Eve were present when punishments were meted out in the garden: I (will) place enmity between you and between the woman, and between your seed and between her seed.

> Gen 21:1, *wyhwh pqd*, and YHWH visited Sarah—he had already visited her before he healed Abimelech.

This observation may have been occasioned by a comparison of Gen 20:17–18 with Gen 18:14. According to the latter, Sarah was to have been a mother within a year. The implication of the former verses is that more than one year had lapsed between Abraham's journey to Gerar, the harem incident, the loss of fertility in Abimelech's household, Abraham's prayer on behalf of Abimelech and his household, and the demonstration of its efficacy. If the

---

[1] All of the following citations from the commentary of Rashi and those below from that of A. Ibn Ezra may be found in any standard edition of their work keyed by chapter and verse.

The sigla "—zz" (= Ziony Zevit) is used throughout this book to mark brief, parenthetical explanatory glosses and clarificatory comments on translations.

divine word in Gen 18:14 was true, then Sarah must have given birth before the women of Abimelech's household, and so the verb *pqd* could only refer to some time before the Gerarites regained their fertility.

Rashi makes similar remarks at Gen 35:29, *wygw'*; 39:1, *wywsp hwrd*; Exod 4:20, *wyqh*; Lev 8:2 concerning *wydbr* in Lev 8:1.

Abraham Ibn Ezra (1089–1164 CE), a more sophisticated linguist and grammarian than Rashi, made similar observations but provided his own rationale:

> Gen 1:9, *wy'mr*, and said—I think that this event is connected to the aforementioned one because the firmament (whose creation is described in vv. 6–8—zz) was not made until the land was dry and the witness (i.e., proof—zz) is "on the day YHWH god made earth and heaven" (Gen 2:4); they were made on the same day. *wkbr 'mr*, and he said already, i.e., and he had said "and let the waters be gathered." And there are hundreds (of examples—zz) like this in the Torah.

> Gen 2:8, *wyt'*, and he planted—*wkbr nt'*, and he already planted, i.e., and he had planted a garden (as indicated in v. 5—zz) in a place called Eden in the east, and now placed the man in it.

> Gen 7:21, *wygw'*, and he died—The meaning of *wygw'* is *kbr gw'*, he died already, i.e., he (i.e., every creature mentioned in this verse—zz) had died (as mentioned in vv. 17–19 describing the extent of the flood—zz). And there are many (examples—zz) in the Torah like it such as *w'thnn* (Deut 3:22) and *wymtr* (Ps 78:24).

> Gen 29: 12, *wygd*, "and he (i.e., Jacob—zz) told Rachel"—(This is placed—zz) late (in the text—zz). Its meaning is that Jacob had already told Rachel, and after (doing that and establishing that they were related—zz) "and he kissed." And there are many examples like it.

Ibn Ezra has similar remarks at Gen 31:24, *wyb'*; 32:23, *wy'br*; 43:28, *wyqdw*; 49:23, *wystmhw*; Exod 4:19, *wy'mr*; 16:15, *wy'mr*; 18:6, *wy'mr*; 28:4, *y'sw*; Lev 9:22, *wyrd*; Ps 78:23–24, *wymtr*.

The comments of both Rashi and Ibn Ezra indicate that they focused on texts as careful exegetes not as grammarians. Their remarks drew attention to the difference between the order in which a text presented events and the intrinsically logical order, according to their perception, in which the events must have occurred.

Contrived examples illustrating this point are the following:

(1a) Max fell.
(1b) John pushed him
(2a) The room was pitch dark.
(2b) Max switched off the light.

If the second sentence of each set is read first, our experience of the world allows us to recognize that the information is provided in the proper causal sequence. However, as presented, it is clear that the event described in the second sentence is anterior to that in the first one.[2]

Rashi and Ibn Ezra did not go beyond this type of observation, drawing attention sporadically to places where time appeared to retrogress even though the narrative advanced within the text. They remarked on passages where they thought that the logical order may not have been apparent to readers.

Some nineteenth century grammarians also drew attention to this phenomenon but addressed it as a grammatical phenomenon. A. Müller listed Gen 2:2; 24:56; 24:62–63; 1 Sam 4:18; and Ps 119:83 as examples of pluperfects.[3] E. König, a gifted and sensitive reader, listed over fifty passages as properly comprehensible only by understanding their verbs as pluperfects.[4]

Using the contrived examples presented above, it is possible to suggest the syllogistic thinking that resulted in this grammatical description. The grammarians confronted two consecutive sentences (1a) John fell. (1b) Max pushed him. Their reasoning may have followed the following pattern: Since the verb in (1b) describes something accomplished before the action described by the past tense verb in verse (1a), it is pluperfect, and is the equivalent of "had pushed him." Hence, sometimes "pushed" should be rendered "had pushed."

The difficulty with this analysis, of course, is that in English, people who wish to use the pluperfect "had pushed" do so. And therefore, when they do not use the pluperfect in utterances, they do not intend to do so; rather, they employ the simple past to indicate two related events out of causal and chronological sequence because the pastness of the events, and that alone, is all that concerns them. They assume that competent listeners will comprehend the proper sequence. Hence, the "pluperfectness" of the second verb is actually a consequence of mental resequencing and interpretation, not of formal grammatical representation.

---

[2] These examples and the following discussion are influenced by the study of A. Lascarides, "Knowledge, causality, and temporal representation," *Linguistics* 30 (1992) 941–44.

[3] A. Müller, *Outlines of Hebrew Syntax* (Glasgow: James Maclehose & Sons, 1882) 15, §18.2; 101–02, §152. (This is a translation of the third part of Müller's, *Hebräische Schulgrammatik*, 1878.)

[4] E. König, *Syntax der hebräischen Sprache* (Leipzig: J. C. Hinrichs Buchhandlung, 1897) 40–43, §115–22.

In his important study of the verbal system, *A Treatise on the Use of the Tenses in Hebrew*, S. R. Driver discussed the pluperfect. Driver included in his analysis of the imperfect *yqtl* with *waw* consecutive a lengthy critique of passages in which *wayyiqtol* forms had been interpreted as pluperfects by exegetes ranging from Ibn Ezra to his own contemporaries. After scrutinizing an inventory of approximately thirty examples, he demonstrated that not one was a clear pluperfect.[5] A corollary of his analysis was the conclusion that only *qatal* forms were used in various collocations that should be translated properly into target European (and other) languages by pluperfects. This was accepted in Gesenius-Kautzsch-Cowley of 1910 which assigned a pluperfect function to some occurrences of *qtl* perfect verbs.[6] Furthermore, G. Bergsträsser, whose 1929 version of *Wilhelm Gesenius' Hebräische Grammatik* is as influential in German speaking countries as Gesenius-Kautzsch-Cowley is in English speaking ones, claimed that since Hebrew had no special form for expressing the pluperfect, *qatal* verbs bore this meaning in various constructions.[7]

Bergsträsser also claimed that *wayyiqtol* forms could express pluperfect when they continued *qatal* forms functioning as pluperfects. He cited Gen 26:18, 31:34; Num 14:36; 1 Sam 28:3; 2 Kgs 23:5 as examples, and referred to "p. 84 ff." of Driver's study.[8] Driver, however, who had discussed only one of these examples, Gen 26:18, wrote that the verb *wystmwm* "is simply the continuation of the verb *ḥprw*," i.e., *wystmwm* is coordinated with *ḥprw*.[9]

Driver's point seems to have been that although one would translate *wystmwm*, "and they had blocked up," according to the conventions of grammatical concord operating in English, Hebrew grammar did not compel this rendering. Accordingly, he discounted the form as a pluperfect. All of

---

[5] S. R. Driver, *A Treatise on the Use of the Tenses in Hebrew* (third revised edition; Oxford: Clarendon, 1892) 22–23, §16; 84–88, §76.

[6] A. E. Cowley, *Gesenius' Hebrew Grammar*, edited and enlarged by E. Kautzsch, translated by A. E. Cowley (second English edition; Oxford: Clarendon, 1910) 310–11, §106f.

[7] G. Bergsträsser, *Hebräische Grammatik II, Teil: Verbum* (Leipzig: J. C. Hinrichs Buchhandlung, 1929) 26–27, §6d.

[8] G. Bergsträsser, *Hebräische Grammatik II*, 27, §6d.

[9] Driver, *A Treatise*, 85.

Bergsträsser's *yiqtol* examples fall into this pattern and may be discounted for the same reason.[10]

A more recent discussion illustrates the importance of distinguishing clearly between the grammar and syntax of the original language, Hebrew, and that of a contemporary target language. In his study of Hebrew verbs, Bo Johnson proposes that *weqatal* verbs in 2 Sam 19:17–19, *wšlḥw*, and *wʿbrh*; 1 Kgs 3:11, *wš'lt*; 1 Kgs 11:10, *wṣwh*; and 2 Kgs 8:10, *whr'ny*; have a pluperfect sense: "Im Kontext ist ein Plusquamperfekt offenbar die richtige Übersetzung, und das *we* Perf ist als Lesart vorzuziehen."[11] However, with regard to 1 Kgs 3:11, he writes:

> Die vorbereitenden Umstände sind hier im Deutschen nicht mit dem Plusquamperfekt, sonders mit dem Perf. wiederzugeben, weil die Erzählung in der Gegenwart spielt.[12]

A similar concern stimulated A. Niccacci's explorations in text linguistics:

> While it is true that Hebrew had only a limited number of verb forms at its disposal, it still seemed odd that, for example, WAYYIQTOL could be translated by virtually all the finite tenses of modern languages as would appear from classical grammars.

He also notes that "the criterion for analysis is not the value of Hebrew verb forms derived from translation into modern languages."[13]

---

[10] B. K. Waltke and M. O'Connor treat the pluperfect most cursorily in their recent study, arguing against Driver that "*wayyqtl* must be understood to represent the pluperfect" (*An Introduction to Biblical Hebrew Syntax* [Winona Lake: Eisenbrauns, 1990] 552–53). Of their three illustrative examples one is coordinated with an earlier *qtl* pluperfect (Num 1:48, cf. vv. 46–47), one is at the beginning of a brief reprise of the narrative line after some long speeches and can be taken as the standard narrative past tense (Exod 4:19), while the third example presents an action in the normal sequence (1 Kgs 13:12—after their father asked the question, the sons went and saw which way the man went) even though it is rendered as a pluperfect in their translation.

[11] "In context, the pluperfect is obviously the correct translation and the *we* Perfect the preferred reading" B. Johnson, *Hebräisches Perfekt und Imperfekt mit vorangehendem we* (Lund: CWK Gleerup, 1971) 41–42. The quotation appears on p. 41. He also cites Gen 28:6, *wšlḥ*; Judg 16:18, *w'lw*. All told, he presents six examples.

The first *waw* of *wšlhw* in 2 Sam 19:18 appears to be a dittograph so that this example may be irrelevant.

[12] The following is a paraphrase: "The verbs cannot be rendered by the German pluperfect but only by the perfect owing to the circumstances of the locution (i.e., the pragmatic context—zz) because the narrative occurs in the present." Johnson, *Hebräisches Perfekt*, 42.

[13] A. Niccacci, *The Syntax of the Verb*, 9, 63.

E. Jenni expresses the problem this way:

> In a dead language with a restricted corpus of texts, the reason for a paradigmatic semantic investigation is practically always given by interlingual comparison.... The practical work is always determined and even biased to some degree by the metalanguage employed by the investigator (English, French, German, modern Hebrew) and it is not wholly indifferent whether a data-base is set up in English, or in French or in Latin.[14]

The observations of Johnson, Niccacci, and Jenni caution that there is nothing natural linguistically or universal psychologically in the organization of the grammars and lexicons of well known modern or ancient languages that may be presupposed as valid automatically in other languages.[15] This is so because all languages relate to the world, but for reasons embedded within the specific cultures that use each language, they segment the world differently. J. Katz suggests that translating between different languages is like comparing "different maps of the same geographic terrain drawn according to different cartographical interests."[16]

We are most familiar with some varied linguistic mappings of the world from comparative anthropological studies of kinship terminology and foods; semantic studies of colors, animal taxonomies, words for precipitation, and "religious" terminology; and linguistic studies of prepositions. Consequently, the caution implicit in the observations of Johnson, Niccacci, and Jenni need not be argued. It is possible to conclude, therefore, that translation provides but limited access to the functions and "meaning(s)" of syntactic structures in source languages.[17]

---

[14] E. Jenni, "Response to P. Swiggers," *ZAH* 6 (1993) 56.

[15] Cf. the discussion of this issue in Z. Zevit, "Talking Funny in Biblical Henglish and Solving a Problem of the YAQTUL Past Tense," *HS* 29 (1988) 25–37 and chapter V below.

[16] J. Katz, *Semantic Theory* (Evanston: Harper and Row, 1972) 346.

[17] This becomes obvious to biblicists when they compare translations in different languages; to grammarians and linguists through contrastive analyses of equivalent grammatical, semantic, and syntactic systems in different languages, e.g., N. Kharma, *A Contrastive Analysis of Verb Forms in English and Arabic* (Heidelburg: Julius Groos, 1983) 44–86; or in different dialects of the same language, e.g., Z. Ben-Hayyim, "Samaritan Hebrew—An Evaluation," (*The Samaritans* [ed. A. D. Crown; Tübingen: J. C. B. Mohr (Paul Siebeck), 1989] 523–25).

J. C. L. Gibson notes that the exigencies of English style made it impossible for even the Authorised Version to indicate the distinctions in the use of the coordinating conjunction ("Coordination by Vav," 278). On a practical level, these insights are experienced affectively by students frustrated by the apparent "illogic" of foreign languages.

E. Y. Kutscher deflected discussion of the pluperfect away from morphology to a different part of the grammar. In his 1982 study of the history of Hebrew, Kutscher mentioned only one way in which Hebrew expressed the pluperfect, "the subject preceding the predicate, e.g., Gen 31:34, *wrḥl lqḥh*, 'and Rachel, meanwhile, had taken....' "[18] The preceding verse relates that Laban entered the tents of Jacob, Leah, and the two handmaids, searching them fruitlessly for his household images. Then he came to the tent of Rachel who had already concealed them in a camel saddle and was sitting on them.

Bergsträsser, along with others, had not missed this verse, but he connected the pluperfect sense with the morphology of the verb, discussing it in a chapter entitled "Bedeutung des einfachen Perfektums" (meaning of the simple perfect). Kutscher, however, connected the exegetical observations of medievalists with the third traditional division of grammar. He implied laconically that the pluperfect sense was indicated by syntax alone. His terse description of the matter, though correct, was incomplete.[19]

---

[18] E. Y. Kutscher, *A History of the Hebrew Language* (Jerusalem: Magnes, 1982) 44, §66. This is mentioned as part of a general statement about the syntax of verbs in what he called "Standard Biblical Hebrew."

M. Z. Kaddari of Bar Ilan University recalls that already in the late 1940s, N. Leibowitz had gathered examples of this phenomena reported by medieval Jewish exegetes for her classes on exegesis and that her mimeographed lists were circulated and discussed in language seminars at the Hebrew University (oral communication, May 30, 1995).

Mr. Shraga Assif of the Hebrew University and the David Yellin College informs me that Kutscher had already shared this observation with his students in the late 60s. I learned of it around the same time attending the lectures of Prof. Ch. Rabin on Biblical Syntax.

Independently, F. I. Andersen described the phenomenon syntactically but did not realize its well defined function, perhaps because he too was influenced by S. R. Driver (*The Sentence in Biblical Hebrew* [The Hague: Mouton, 1974] 79–82, 85–86 and cf. note 5).

T. Muraoka, a graduate of the Hebrew University, restates Kutscher's position but does not go beyond it (P. Joüon and T. Muraoka, *A Grammar of Biblical Hebrew* [Roma: Pontificio Istituto Biblica, 1991] 390–91, §118d).

[19] R. Buth, considering this matter from the vantage of Text Linguistics, describes it as "temporal overlay," a yo-yoing in the narrative's chronology that overlays a time segment already covered by another section of narrative ("Methodological Collision Between Source Criticism and Discourse Analysis: The Problem of 'Unmarked Temporal Overlay' and the Pluperfect/Nonsequential wayyiqtol," *Biblical Hebrew and Discourse Linguistics* [ed. R. D. Bergen; USA: Summer Institute of Linguistics, 1994] 138–39). Buth, however, uses this term to cover all sorts of repetitions at different levels in the text, including *Wiederaufnahme* and various text cohesive devices of a chronologically insignificant nature, and so renders it inappropriate for this study (pp. 142–44, 150). His study is more in the tradition of exegesis than of grammatical analysis.

III

THE ANTERIOR CONSTRUCTION

When authors of narrative prose wished to indicate unambiguously 1) *pluperfect*, i.e., that a given action in the past had *commenced and concluded* before another action in the past, or 2) *preperfect*, i.e., that a given action in the past had *commenced but not necessarily terminated* in the past prior to the beginning of another action, they employed a particular construction to express this sequencing, a type of circumstantial clause. These clauses consist of a subject, noun or pronoun, followed by a *qatal* past tense. (The *qatal* verb distinguishes these clauses both formally and semantically from similar clauses with participles whose time referent is that of the verb in the preceding clause.) They are appended to a preceding clause by *waw* conjunctive. In some cases, this connection is partially obfuscated by the verse length constraints of the masoretic reading/cantillation tradition, intrusive verse numbers, interlinear chapter divisions, and the division of the text into *pisqā'ōt*.

The structure of these clauses is w^e + *S(ubject)* + *qatal*. **However, the necessary condition for their realization is a past tense verb, $(w)yqtl$ or qtl, in the narrative of the preceding clause.**[1]

This condition excludes 1) the form *wyhy*, "and it was," which is sometimes the equivalent of *whnh*, "and lo" (e.g., Gen 22:1; 40:1; Ruth 1:1a), when

---

[1] This descriptive statement was developed after considering hundreds of passages within which events were ostensibly narrated out of chronological sequence.

The general structure of these clauses, but not the conditions and restrictions under which they are realized, was pointed out by M. Fruchtman, "A Few Notes on the Study of Biblical Narrative," *Ha-Sifrut/Literature* no. 22, VI/2 (1976) 63–64 (Hebrew) and E. Rubinstein, *Contemporary Hebrew and Ancient Hebrew* (Hebrew; Israel: Ministry of Defense, 1980) 20, 22–23.

Genesis 29:17, for example, has this structure but does not meet the first condition. The verb is a simple past, not pluperfect.

it functions as a presentative, not as a verb. 2) It excludes verbs in parenthetical, inserted sentences that interrupt main narrative flow, i.e., that are off the main narrative line. (This point is illustrated in some examples presented below.) 3) It also excludes participles which, although often rendered as past tense verbs in European languages, are actually substantives and therefore irrelevant to this analysis.[2]

Recognizing the dedicated nature of the anterior construction enables the comprehension of compositional subtlety in many biblical passages and engenders an appreciation for one of the ways in which the ancient authors solved a problem that hindered them in their representation of reality (or verisimilitudes of reality).[3] The distinction introduced between the pluperfect and the preperfect in the following examples is useful heuristically because 1) it is only through the pluperfect examples that the construction is recognized unambiguously in context, and 2) some of the preperfect examples are more difficult to analyze and to render into English because of English usage. Possibly, many preperfects could be translated quite comfortably into other languages with no such difficulty for a variety of reasons. In Hebrew, as will be seen, no formal distinction exists between the pluperfect and preperfect examples.

The following examples are sometimes glossed and/or provided with a brief explanatory comment.

A. Pluperfect

1. Genesis 6:7–8

ויאמר יהוה אמחה את האדם אשר בראתי מעל פני האדמה...,
ונח מצא חן בעיני יהוה

And YHWH said, "I will wipe the people that I created from the surface of the earth…," *wnḥ mṣʼ ḥn*, and/but Noah had found favor in the eyes of YHWH.

---

[2] The time reference semantic of participles in biblical Hebrew and attendant problems is described and analyzed by A. Gordon, "The Development of the Participle in Biblical, Mishnaic, and Modern Hebrew," *Afroasiatic Linguistics* 8/3 (1982) 2–10.

[3] Selection of the adjective "anterior" to describe this construction is influenced by its application in J. Bybee, R. Perkins, W. Pagliuca, *The Evolution of Grammar. Tense, Aspect and Modality in the Languages of the World* (Chicago: University of Chicago Press, 1994) 54: an anterior "signals that the situation occurs prior to reference time and is relevant to the situation at reference time."

Comment: These curt verses introducing a more detailed story of the flood indicate that Noah had found favor in the eyes of YHWH before he determined to destroy humanity.

This is clear in Gen 6:9–13 where the events are ordered sequentially: Noah the pious "walks with YHWH," Noah has children, the earth corrupts itself and is filled with violence, YHWH orders Noah—who has obviously found favor in his eyes prior to the warning—to prepare himself for the coming catastrophe and announces that he has determined to put an end to mankind.

2. Genesis 7:18–19

ויגברו המים וירבו מאד על הארץ ותלך התבה על פני המים, והמים גברו מאד מאד על הארץ ויכסו כל ההרים הגבהים אשר תחת כל השמים.

And the waters rose and increased greatly over the land, and the ark floated on the surface of the water, *whmym gbrw m'd m'd*, and the waters had risen very much over the earth and they covered all the high mountains that are under all the heavens.

Comment: Genesis 7:17 alone seems to indicate that after much rain, the ark barely floated: "And the deluge was on the earth forty days, and the waters became very plentiful and they bore the ark, and it rose from the earth." In fact, the ark could only float safely and freely after all obstacles were well beneath its displacement depth; similarly, only after the waters rose over the highest points of land on which life forms could stand, even neck deep, could the death notice of v. 21 have made sense: "All flesh that crawls on the land perished: fowl, domestic animals, wild animals, every swarming creature that swarms on the earth, and all humans."

3. Genesis 13:12–14

אברם ישב בארץ כנען ולוט ישב בערי הככר ויאהל עד סדם—ואנשי סדם רעים וחטאים ליהוה מאד—ויהוה אמר אל אברם אחרי הפרד לוט מעמו שא נא עיניך וראה....

Abram settled in the land of Canaan *wlwṭ yšb*, and/but Lot had settled among the cities of the plain and he tented up to Sodom (where he settled—zz), ...[4] *wyhwh 'mr 'l 'brm*, but YHWH had said to Abram after Lot separated from him, "Lift up your eyes and see...."

---

[4] The verbless circumstantial clause in v.13, *w'nšy sdwm...lyhwh m'd*, describes the people of Sodom at the very time that Lot had contact with them.

Comment: The main narrative line in the pericope skips from v. 11 to v. 18. Verse 12 refers to something that took place before Abram settled and anticipates Genesis 14. Lot settled in Sodom before Abram settled in Eloney Mamre (cf. v. 18). Verse 14 indicates that before Abraham settled, before Lot settled in or near Sodom, even as Lot was wending his way down the mountains to the well-watered plain by the Dead Sea, YHWH promised the land to Abraham. Verses 12–13 indicate that the J tradition knew the story of Genesis 14.

4. Genesis 15:17

ויהי השמש באה, ועלטה היה....

And lo, the sun set, *w'lṭh hyh*, and/but there had been darkness (even before the sunset, a reference to v. 12 where "a great darkness fell on Abraham as the sun was about to set"—zz).

Comment: Had the narrative wished to indicate that the darkness came about as a result of the sunset, it would have read, *hšmš b'h wyhy 'lṭh*, "and the sun set and there was darkness."

5. Genesis 15:18–16:1

ביום ההוא כרת יהוה את אברם ברית לאמר לזרעך נתתי את הארץ הזאת...
ושרי אשת אברם לא ילדה לו...

On that day YHWH made a covenant with Abram saying, "I give this land to your seed...," *wśry 'št 'brm l' yldh*, and/but Sarai, wife of Abram, had not borne for him....

6. Genesis 20:3–4

ויבא אלהים אל אבימלך בחלום הלילה ויאמר לו הנך מת על האשה אשר
לקחת...,, ואבימלך לא קרב אליה....

And God came to Abimelech in a night dream and said, "You are dead on account of the woman that you took...," *w'bymlk l' qrb 'lyh*, and/but Abimelech had not approached her (before the dream of v. 3—zz).[5]

---

[5] The author could have expressed the negative without a pluperfect by writing *wl' qrb 'lyh*, "and he did not approach her," at the end of v. 2.

7. Genesis 20:17–21:1a

ויתפלל אברהם אל האלהים וירפא אלהים את אבימלך ואת אשתו
ואמהתיו וילדו.... ויהוה פקד את שרה כאשר אמר....

And Abraham prayed to God and God healed Abimelech and his wife and his handmaidens and they gave birth..., *wyhwh pqd 't śrh*, and/but YHWH had visited Sarah (sometime between the events of Gen 18:14 and 20:18, a period of almost a year—zz) as he said.[6]

Comment: This example, one of those commented on by Rashi, is discussed above in chapter II.

8. Genesis 38:24b–25

ויאמר יהודה הוציאוה ותשרף. הוא מוצאת, והיא שלחה אל חמיה לאמר....

...and Judah said, "Take her out and let her be burnt." She was taken out, *why' šlḥh*, and/but she had sent to her father-in-law (a messenger bearing his tokens and a cryptic message after he had ordered her execution in v. 24 but before it was implemented—zz) saying....

Comment: Verse 26, a last minute confession by Judah exonerating Tamar, was triggered by her understated presentation of forensic evidence. The story fails to explain how Judah canceled the order. Information completing the narrative could have come between v. 26 and v. 27.

9. Exodus 9:23

ויט משה את מטהו על השמים, ויהוה נתן קלת וברד, ותהלך אש ארצה
וימטר יהוה ברד על ארץ מצרים.

And Moses extended his staff to the heavens, *wyhwh ntn qlt wbrd*, and YHWH had set thunder and hail (before Moses did so, cf. v. 22—zz), and fire went earthward, and YHWH rained hail on the land of Egypt.

Comment: In verse 22, Moses was instructed "extend your hand heavenward and there will be hail in all the land of Egypt...." The story presupposes that hail is unnatural in Egypt and the pluperfect clause in the next verse clarifies how it got there. Verse 23 indicates that YHWH, in preparation for this plague, set or placed thunder and hail (in the heavens) before Moses extended

---

[6] In the extant text, the pluperfect bridges between the main E narrative (i.e., Gen 20:1–17) and J (i.e., Gen 21:1a, 2a). Thematically, it connects the wives and handmaidens of Abimelech to women of similar status in Abraham's household and refocuses attention to the drama of Abraham's progeny.

his staff. The meteorological display was then initiated by a fiery flash followed by a rain of hail on the land of Egypt.

10. Exodus 33:6–7

ויתנצלו בני ישראל את עדים...ומשה יקח את האהל ונטה לו מחוץ
למחנה הרחק מן המחנה....

And the children of Israel stripped off their ornaments..., *wmšh yqḥ*, and/but Moses had taken[7] the tent *wnṭh lw*, and had pitched it outside the camp, far from the camp....

Comment: In Exod 33:5 the people were threatened: "...you are a stiff necked people. One moment, and I will come up in your midst, *bqrbk*, and I will destroy you; now, remove your ornaments from yourselves and I will decide what I will do to you."

The tent had been taken from the center of the Israelite encampment after the threat of v. 5 but before Israelites removed their ornaments. Moses moved the place of imminent theophany far from the source of YHWH's anger and then negotiated a reprieve for the people on the basis of his personal store of good will, vv. 12–16. (Verses 8–11 constitute a parenthetical aside that stands outside of the main story line.) In the meantime, the people, having removed their ornaments, waited until their fate was decided.

11. Numbers 5:13–14

ושכב איש אתה שכבת זרע ונעלם מעיני אישה ונסתרה והיא נטמאה, ועד אין
בה, והוא לא נתפשה; ועבר עליו רוח קנאה וקנא את אשתו, והוא נטמאה,
או עבר עליו רוח קנאה וקנא את אשתו, והיא לא נטמאה.

And a man lay with her carnally and it was hidden from the eyes of her husband and it (i.e., *škbh*, the laying, a grammatically feminine noun—zz) was undetected, *why' nṭm'h*, and/but she had become impure; and there being no witness against her, *why' l' ntpśh*, and she had not been caught; and a spirit of jealousy overcame him (i.e., her husband—zz) and he was jealous concerning his wife, *why' nṭm'h*, and she had become impure, or a spirit of jealousy overcame him and he was jealous concerning his wife, *why' l' nṭm'h*, and/but she had not become impure.[8]

---

[7] The verb *yqḥ* is taken either as the past tense of a verb *y-q-ḥ*, a variant form of *l-q-ḥ*, or as an error.

[8] Verse 13 could also be translated "a man lay with her carnally, and he (i.e., the man—zz) hid himself from the eyes of her husband, and (she) concealed herself—and she (in the state of—zz) having become impure...."

Comment: The trigger for the judicial procedure is the "spirit of jealousy" in v. 14a which may or may not have been justified. Verse 13 deals with two distinct matters: impurity and arrest. According to the internal logic of v. 13, her becoming impure was a concomitant of the man lying with her in private; her not being caught was attendant to the fact that there had been no witnesses. This transpired *prior* to her husband seeing her and suspecting that she may have engaged in illicit sex, and certainly *prior* to his discovering whether or not his suspicion was justified.

Impurity is mentioned in both verses because the husband thought that he could sense a miasmic impurity adhering to her person. However, having eliminated all likely and obvious sources for such impurity, he was left only with a festering suspicion that she had committed adultery.

12. Judges 3:25–26

ויחילו עד בוש, והנה איננו פתח דלתות העליה. ויקחו את המפתח ויפתחו והנה
אדניהם נפל ארצה מת, ואהוד נמלט עד התמהמהם, והוא עבר את הפסילים
וימלט השעירתה.

And they waited until embarrassed, and lo, he isn't opening the doors of the chamber, and they took the key and opened, and lo, their master fallen dead on the ground, *w'hd nmlṭ*, and Ehud had fled (as described in vv. 22–23—zz) while they tarried, *whw' 'br*, and he had passed the quarries, and he escaped to Ha-seirat.

13. 1 Samuel 4:18

...ויפל מעל הכסא אחרנית...וימת כי זקן האיש וכבד, והוא שפט את ישראל
ארבעים שנה.

...and he fell backwards from the chair...and he died because the man was old and heavy, *whw' špṭ 't yśr'l*, and he had judged Israel for forty years.

14. 1 Samuel 25:20–21

...והנה דוד ואנשיו ירדים לקראתה ותפגש אתם, ודוד אמר....
...and behold, David and his men coming toward her and she (i.e., Abigail —zz) met them, *wdwd 'mr*, and David had thought (all that is presented in vv. 21–22 about destroying the ingrate Nabal, whose property David had protected, and his household before he met Abigail—zz)....

15. 2 Samuel 18:17–18

ויקחו את אבשלום וישליבו אתו ביער אל הפחת הגדול ויצבו עליו גל אבנים
גדול מאד—וכל ישראל נסו איש לאהלו—ואבשלם לקח ויצב לו בחיו את
מצבת....

And they took Absalom and cast him in the forest into a great pit and they set up over him (i.e., Absalom—zz) a very large heap of stones, *wkl yśr'l nsw*, and all Israel had fled, each man to his tent, *w'bšlm lqh wyṣb*, and Absalom had taken and had set up for himself during his lifetime a stele....

B. Preperfect

1. Genesis 2:25–3:1

ויהיו שניהם ערומים, האדם ואשתו, ולא יתבששו. והנחש היה ערום מכל
חית השדה אשר עשה יהוה אלהים ויאמר אל האשה....

And the two of them were both naked, the man and his wife, but were not ashamed of each other, *whnḥš hyh ʿrwm*, and the snake had been the most crafty of all the animals of the field which YHWH Elohim made (as a helpmate for the man in Gen 2:18–20—zz), and he said to the woman....

Comment: The nature of the snake and his superiority over the others was determined or established even before the woman came on the scene. The particular characteristic with which the snake was abundantly endowed, encapsulated by the word *ʿrwm*, involved the ability to plan realistically for his own benefit and to avoid trouble (Prov 13:16; 14:8, 18; 22:3; 27:12). It was mentioned here, however, because it cued the audience to attend carefully to the following conversation which would hardly be as casual and innocent as it may have appeared.

In English, the translation, "had been crafty," may be taken as implying that at some time in the past, the snake had ceased being crafty; that is not implied by the Hebrew. Unfortunately, there is no way of avoiding the inelegant woodenness of the English without paraphrasing or mistranslating other parts of the verse, e.g., "...from all the animals of the field that YHWH Elohim *had* made...." When considered along with the definition of *preperfect* provided in the first paragraph of this chapter, the translation may be tolerated as a heuristic one. The difficulties imposed by this and some of the following examples on the English translator are considered below in chapter V.

2. Genesis 4:2

...ויהי הבל רעה צאן וקין היה עבד אדמה.

...And Abel was a shepherd, *wqyn hyh*, and/but Cain had been a worker of the soil.

Comment: Cain, who was older, began his work as an agriculturalist before Abel embarked on his career as a pasturalist. Obviously, once Abel engaged in his profession, both were gainfully employed. The extant text may be contrasted with hypothetical alternatives: the first with a repeated verb, *wyhy hbl rʿh-ṣʾn wyhy qyn ʿwbd ʾdmh*, "and Abel was a shepherd and Cain was a worker of the soil"; the second having a gapped verb, *wyhy hbl rʿh-ṣʾn wqyn ʿwbd ʾdmh*, "and Abel was a shepherd and Cain a worker of the soil."

3. Genesis 4:3–4

ויהי מקץ ימים, ויבא קין מפרי האדמה מנחה ליהוה; והבל הביא, גם הוא,
מבכרות צאנו....

And it was at the end of a season, and Cain brought a gift for YHWH from the fruit of the ground, *whbl hby' gm hw'*, and/but Abel, even he, had also brought from the firstlings of his flock...

Comment: The situation here is identical to that in the previous example except that the characters are reversed. Yes, Cain brought an offering, but it was Abel who had presented one or started to present one earlier. (According to the first possibility the verb could be considered a pluperfect, according to the second, a preperfect.) The clause indicates that Abel was first.

4. Genesis 14:17–19

ויצא מלך סדם לקראתו אחרי שובו...ומלכי צדק מלך שלם הוציא לחם ויין,
והוא כהן לאל עליון, ויברכהו....

And the king of Sodom came out towards him after his return..., *wmlkyṣdq mlk šlm hwṣy' lḥm wyyn*, and Melchizedek, king of Shalem, had brought out bread and wine, he (being) a priest to El Elyon, and he blessed him....

Comment: Melchizedek's act preceded but overlapped that of the king of Sodom. This clarifies why Melchizedek was the first to greet him in vv. 19–20.

5. Genesis 19:23–24

השמש יצא על הארץ ולוט בא צערה ויהוה המטיר על סדם ועל עמרה גפרית
ואש....

The sun rose over the earth, *wlwṭ b'*, and Lot had come to Zoar, *wyhwh hmṭyr*, and YHWH had rained fire and sulfur on Sodom and Gomorrah....

Comment: Lot's arrival at Zoar and the destruction of Sodom both took place before sunrise. The first verb is preperfect, the second pluperfect.

This clarifies the angel's remark in v. 22 which, at first blush, appears to mean that nothing would happen until Lot arrived at Zoar. Recognizing the preperfect in 19:23–24 clarifies that the author intended the expression *'d bw'k* in v. 22 to mean "until your coming," i.e., closer to there than to here, and not "until after your arrival." The latter would have been expressed by *'d 'ḥry bw'k*.

6. Genesis 26:25–26

...ויכרו שם עבדי יצחק באר, ואבימלך הלך אליו מגרר....

...and Isaac's servants dug a well there, *w'bymlk hlk 'lyw mgrr*, and Abimelech had walked to him from Gerar....

Comment: Abimelech and his company had set out before Isaac's servants started their labor. Either the well itself came in or information that it had come in reached Isaac on the day that Abimelech visited him but after Abimelech had departed for home (cf. v. 32).

7. Genesis 27:5–6

...וילך עשו השדה לצוד ציד...ורבקה אמרה אל יעקב בנה....

...and Esau went to the field to hunt game..., *wrbqh 'mrh 'l y'qb*, and/but Rebekah had said to Jacob her son....

Comment: Rebekah had apparently concocted her ruse even while overhearing Isaac's request of Esau, v. 5a, and she began to implement it even before Esau set off to hunt.

One source of dramatic tension in the story is the lingering doubt whether or not Rebekah and Jacob could complete their deception before Esau's return. These verses emphasize the narrowness of the time margin available for executing the plan (cf. Gen 27:30).

8. Genesis 31:47

ויקרא לו לבן יגר שהדותא ויעקב קרא לו גלעד.

And Laban called it Yegar Shahadutha, *wy'qb qr' lw*, but Jacob had called it Gal-Ed.

Comment: Use of the preperfect here indicates that Jacob had named the place in Hebrew before Laban named it in Aramaic.

9. Exodus 19:2–3

ויסעו מרפידים ויבאו מדבר סיני, ויחנו במדבר, ויחן שם ישראל נגד ההר,
ומשה עלה אל האלהים....

And they traveled from Rephidim and they came to the Sinai wilderness, and they camped in the wilderness, and Israel encamped opposite the mountain, *wmšh 'lh*, and/but Moses had gone up to God....

Comment: Moses did not ascend the mountain prior to the arrival of the Israelites at Sinai. After they arrived and began setting up the camp, he began his ascent. The construction creates a split screen image: Moses ascending the mountain as the Israelites set up camp.

10. Exodus 20:21

ויעמד העם מרחק ומשה נגש אל הערפל אשר שם האלהים.

And the people stood far off, *wmšh ngš*, and/but Moses had approached the darkness where God was.

Comment: In v. 18, the people who had been pressing in at the foot of the mountain were so overwhelmed by the theophany that they withdrew. Despite Moses' admonition not to fear (v. 20), they remained where they were at a safe distance. Verse 21 contrasts between Moses advancing and the people standing far off.

The fact that *'md*, "stand," is an intransitive verb makes this a difficult example to comprehend.

11. Joshua 8:20

ויפנו אנשי העי אחריהם ויראו והנה עלה עשן העיר השמימה ולא היה בהם
ידים לנוס הנה והנה, והעם הנס המדבר נהפך אל הרודף.

And the people of Ai turned behind them (i.e., looked backwards—zz) and saw and behold, the smoke of the city ascended to the sky and there was no strength in them to flee here or there, *wh'm hns hmdbr nhpk*, and the people (seemingly—zz) fleeing to the wilderness had turned back towards the pursuers.

Comment: The combination of impressions caused initially by their comprehension of the significance of the smoke behind them and then by the changed direction of those whom they had thought that they were pursuing led to Aiite consternation and paralysis. Since their concern with fleeing could only have developed after assessing that they were trapped in a pincer movement, Israelite forces must have reversed direction prior to the Aiite collapse.

12. Judges 10:18–11:1

ויאמרו העם...מי האיש אשר יחל להלחם בבני עמון יהיה לראש לכל ישבי
גלעד, ויפתח הגלעדי היה גבור חיל....

And the people said...whoever be the man that begins to fight against the sons of Ammon, he will become the head of all inhabitants of Gilead, *wyptḥ hgl'dy hyh gbwr*, and Jephthah the Gileadite had been a mighty warrior (even before the circumstances of Judg 10:7–17 transpired—zz)....

Syntactically, anterior clauses are connected to the narrative flow through the conjunction which creates formally a minimal cohesion; semantically, they are disconnected because they introduce a new topic; but logically, they work against text cohesiveness by arresting and reversing temporarily the chronological flow of the narrative. Their main function is to provide information for the main narrative line by advancing heretofore unknown background information into the foreground.[9] In some cases, the information can be trivial, as in death notices (Judg 4:1; 16:31); in others, it can be significant, marking the incipit of motifs that then come to dominate the narrative (Gen 6:7–8; 37:2–3); in yet others, it may be of a parenthetical nature (Gen 8:4–5; 31:25).

A comparison of how five commonly used translations rendered the above 27 examples is illuminating: *King James Version, New American Bible, New English Bible, New Jewish Publication Society* translation, and the *New Revised Standard Version*. All five provided a pluperfect translation of the relevant verbs in Gen 20:3–4, 1 Sam 4:18, 1 Sam 25:20–21, and 2 Sam 18:17–18, presented above as "pluperfect" examples ##6, 13, 14, and 15 respectively. In addition, the NAB, NEB, and NJPS did so in Gen 15:18–16:1, example #5; and the NAB and NJPS in Judg 3:25–26, example #12. Only the NEB recognized it in Gen 6:7–8, example #1. Of the 12 examples presented above as "preperfects," only one, Gen 26:25–26, example #6 was so translated, and that only by the NAB.[10]

Of these five versions, the NAB and, to a lesser extent, the NJPS and NRSV appear to have been sensitive to some chronological displacement in many of the texts, particularly in those listed above as "preperfects." These were handled in translation either through paraphrase, rearranging the verse, or by expressing the notion of a frequent, regular, or simultaneous activity through words and expressions such as "while, during, used to."[11]

Generalizing from this limited survey of five versions, it is clear that they cannot be used to gauge the presence or absence of an anterior construction in the Hebrew text. This follows practically from the aforegoing observations, and theoretically from the discussion in chapter II about why translations cannot be used to discern the sense of underlying verb forms.

---

[9] Cf. R. Longacre, "Discourse Peak as Zone of Turbulence," *Beyond the Sentence, Discourse and Sentential Form* (ed. J. Wirth; Ann Arbor: Karoma, 1985) 81–98; Niccacci, *The Syntax of the Verb*, 35–37, 48. Niccacci's observations about these clauses are correct but incomplete.

[10] I thank Dr. T. Fretheim for drawing my attention to the NAB's renderings.

[11] The reason why this selection of adverbial expressions is particularly appropriate for rendering the preperfect examples is clarified by the discussion below in chapter V.

*A list of verses with the anterior construction indicating a **pluperfect** relationship:*[12]

Gen 1:1–2ᵃ; 1:5ᵇ; 3:24–4:1 (cf. 4:17); 6:7–8; 7:19; 8:4–5; 13:12–13; 15:17; 16:1; 20:3–4; 20:18–21:1; 24:1; 24:16; 24:61–62; 25:33–34aᶜ; 26:27; 31:17–19ᵈ; 31:25; 31:33–34; 33:16–17; 34:4–5; 34:6–7; 37:2–3; 37:11ᵉ; 37:35–36; 38:14; 38:25; 38:30–39:1; 41:56–57; 42:22–23; 42:38–43:1; 48:9–10;

Exod 9:23; 10:13a (cf. vv. 4b–5); 14:29; 15:19; 33:6–7;

Num 1:47; 5:13–14; 13:22; 13:30–31ᶠ; 21:25–26; 27:3;

Josh 2:4b–6 (cf. 4a); 3:15; 3:16; 3:18–19; 4:17–19; 8:21; 18:1;

Judg 3:18–19; 3:20ᵍ; 3:25–26; 4:1; 4:15–17; 16:31; 19:10–11ʰ;

1 Sam 1:5; 3:7; 4:10–11, 13; 4:18; 4:22–5:1ⁱ; 9:14–15; 13:3, 4, 5, 6, 7ʲ; 19:17–18; 25:20–21; 28:2–3; 30:3;

2 Sam 2:28–29; 2:28–30; 3:28–30; 4:2; 4:4; 18:17–18;

1 Kgs 1:41; 2:28; 2:32ᵏ; 11:21; 22:30–31;

2 Kgs 3:3–4; 4:30–31; 6:32; 7:16–17; 8:29b; 9:1ˡ; 9:14; 9:16; 9:27; 17:29–31;

Cant 5:6;

Esth 3:15–4:1aᵐ; 6:4; 8:1; 8:14–15.[13]

Comments:

a) Gen 1:1–2. This verse is a valid example only if *br'* is interpreted as a 3 m.s. verb, "he created." It would mean that the stuff which Elohim worked on in creating what came to be identified as "the earth" had been unformed and void before Elohim acted. Were the clause intended to be purely circumstantial, it would have been written *wh'rṣ thw wbhw*, "the earth, unformed and void."[14] If, however, *b-r-'* is interpreted with most modern exegetes as a construct infinitive, then this verse is not relevant to the discussion.

---

[12] Raised letters next to a verse number refer to comments below.

[13] Despite these examples, the typical pattern does not indicate anteriority consistently in the book, e.g., Esth 7:6–8; 8:1; 9:2; 9:15–16. This is a consequence of Esther's post-exilic date. The syntax of Esther no longer follows the typical patterning of pre-exilic prose; it reflects the modifications and innovations accepted by Hebrew literati during the fifth-fourth centuries BCE. Cf. Kutscher, *A History of the Hebrew Language*, 45, 74, 81; Joüon-Muraoka, *A Grammar of Biblical Hebrew*, 9–10 and the literature cited, and the brief remarks about the transition from classical to mishnaic Hebrew in chapter VII below.

[14] I thank Dr. R. Westbrook who suggested this example to me.

b) Gen 1:5. The pre-existing darkness had been named earlier (cf. v. 2), inasmuch as the darkness, i.e., night, existed before the light, i.e., day.[15]

c) Gen 25:33–34a. The implication of these verses is that Jacob fed Esau and, while the latter ate, offered to purchase the birthright. Contrary to the common perception, the grammar indicates that the sale was neither coerced nor made under duress. Compare Gen 27:36 where the first *l-q-ḥ* referring to the birthright may be a commercial term.

d) Gen 31:17–19d. "And Laban had gone to shear his sheep" while Jacob set out to return to Canaan (vv. 17–18). Verses 20–21 continue the normal narrative sequence even though they are in the same pluperfect time frame. Verse 22 continues the narrative of v. 18.

e) Gen 37:11. Even before the brothers became jealous, Jacob had noted the significance of the dreams.

f) Num 13:30–31. Caleb's assertion in v. 30b that the people should go up into the land and that they would inherit it because they were able does not respond to anything reported by the spies in vv. 27–29. Rather, it addresses their statement in v. 31, "we are unable to go up to the people (in the land) because they are stronger than us." Furthermore, the opaque expression in v. 30a, "and Caleb silenced the people *'l mšh*, to/for Moses," suggests that Moses was somehow involved with the Israelite complaint. His involvement is first mentioned explicitly in Num 14:2: "and all the children of Israel complained against Moses and against Aaron...."

The anterior construction in v. 31, "and the people who had gone up with him...had said," indicates that the contents of their remarks in vv. 31–33 were heard before Caleb's response in v. 30.

Since the whole section, Num 13:27–14:4 is attributed to a single source, J, the placement of v. 30 in the middle of the spies' report may be considered from the perspective of rhetoric. Verse 30 divides the report into roughly two sections of equal length. In addition, both vv. 30 and 31 employ *'-l-h* and *y-k-l*.

g) Judg 3:20. The "natural" sequence of events in this section of the narrative is confusing and may be due, in part, to faulty editing. Verse 20 would have Ehud approaching Eglon even before the retainers had left the room.

---

15 Cf. also A. Niccacci, "Analysis of Biblical Narrative," *Biblical Hebrew and Discourse Linguistics* (ed. R. D. Bergen; USA: Summer Institute of Linguistics, 1994) 181–83. Niccacci reaches a similar conclusion on the basis of his text linguistic analysis.

Perhaps it is intended to parallel v. 19, i.e., the secret matter was a word/matter of the deity.

h) Judg 19:10–11. These verses are difficult to interpret. From v. 10b up through the city name, *ybws*, in v. 11a, they contain some parenthetical material. In v. 11a, *yrd* should be read rather than *rd*.

i) 1 Sam 4:22–5:1. The Philistines took the ark (cf. 1 Sam 5:1) long before the news was brought to Shiloh (cf. 1 Sam 4:11). Phineas' wife started to labor and gave birth only after she learned about the capture of the ark, the death of her husband, and the death of her father-in-law.

j) 1 Sam 13:3, 4, 5, 6, 7. These verses have proven troublesome to translate and to interpret. In part, this is because they contain grammatical infelicities and other scribal corruptions that are treated as a matter of course in critical commentaries and, in part, because they employ the anterior construction whose informational import has not been understood. Recognizing that the anterior construction was employed in this section, perhaps to emphasize the exciting confusion of simultaneous events, helps alleviate some of the difficulties.

The actual sequence of events appears to have been the following: Saul blew the *shofar* signaling revolt; Jonathan slew the Philistine governor (v. 3); Israel heard of the slaying; Philistines mustered and gathered to fight; Israelites rallied to Saul at Gilgal. As the Philistines were gathering, other Israelites dug into hiding even as yet another group, designated "*Ibrim*," fled (vv. 6, 7).

k) 1 Kgs 2:32. David had not known of Joab's plan to kill the "two good and righteous people" before it was executed.

l) 2 Kgs 9:1. The events of 2 Kgs 9:1–13 were inserted editorially into a story that continues from 8:29 at 9:14 with a resumptive repetition. Thus the events of 9:1 began before the king of Israel and Judah met at Jezreel and run parallel to their meeting. Elisha's activities began prior to the wounding of the king of Israel.

m) Esth 3:15–4:1a. Royal couriers were dispatched to the provinces bearing multiple copies of the decrees that Haman issued concerning the Jews in Esth 3:13. At v. 15, the author reprises their dispatch, describing what occurred in Shushan where the decree had been issued even before their hurried departure. Even before they left, the king and Haman sat to drink—*yšbw* has a preperfect sense here—and continued imbibing even as the couriers rode off to the corners of the kingdom, but Mordecai had already known all that transpired.

*A list of verses with the anterior construction indicating a **preperfect**
relationship:*

>   Gen 2:25–3:1; 4:2; 4:3–4; 11:3; 14:17–18; 19:4; 19:23–24; 25:33–
>   34; 26:25–26; 27:5–6; 27:30; 31:47; 32:1–2; 33:16–17; 41:56–57;
>   42:8; 45:14; 45:15–16;
>   Exod 2:25–31; 2:25–3:1; 19:2–3; 20:21;
>   Josh 8:15; 8:18–19; 8:20;
>   Judg 4:10–11; 4:15–16; 10:18–11:1; 15:14; 18:22;
>   1 Sam 12:2;
>   2 Sam 10:13–14; 13:36–37;
>   1 Kgs 19:3–4; 1 Kgs 20:34–35;
>   2 Kgs 5:24–25; 7:2–3; 9:23–24; 9:30–31; 20:4;
>   Jonah 3:3;
>   Cant 5:4; 5:5.

One example of the preperfect type is found in the Siloam Tunnel Inscription,
ca. 705–01 BCE (*KAI* 189:5–6):

>   *...wylkw hmym mn hmwṣ' 'l hbrkh bm'tym* [w]*'lp 'mh wm*[*'*]*t 'mh hyh gbh
>   hṣr 'l r'š hḥṣb*[*m*]...
>
>   ...And the waters flowed from the source to the pool, two hundred and one
>   thousand cubits; and o[ne hundr]ed cubits had been the height of the rock
>   above the heads of the excavator[s]...

Comments:

This example is formally correct, but somewhat anomalous. The grammatical gender of the verb is masculine, rendering it congruent with the predicate
adjective *gbh* but not with the subject *m*[*'*]*t 'mh*. The height of the rock had
been and continued to be one hundred cubits above the head of a person in the
tunnel.

Perhaps this remark indicates that those excavating the horizontal tunnel
followed a natural fissure one hundred cubits below the surface and kept low-
ering it until they reached a level where the water flowed. This would account
for the observable fact that at some points the ceiling of the tunnel is so low
that one must stoop to walk through whereas at others the ceiling is far over-
head.

The anterior construction, as described above, is not an idiosyncratic innovation in Hebrew narrative. The 9th century BCE Moabite inscription of Mesha provides three examples:[16]

1) Lines 7–8

> I saw (my way) with him and with his (i.e., Omri's) house, *wyšr'l 'bd 'bd 'lm*, but Israel had utterly perished/been destroyed for ever.

Comment: This indicates that before Mesha dealt with Omri and his house, a phrase referring to resident Israelite officials among whom scions of Omri were found, he destroyed the soldier-tribesmen of Israel.

2) Lines 9–10

> And I built Qiryaten, *w'š gd yšb*, and the men of Gad had dwelt in the land of Atarot for ever (i.e., a long time before I built Qiryaten—zz).

3) Lines 18–19

> I took from there [altars] of YHWH and I dragged them before Kemosh, *wmlk yšr'l bnh*, and the king of Israel had built Yahas, and he dwelt in it when he fought me.[17]

---

[16] Lines 1–2 of the inscription cannot be pluperfect: *'by mlk 'l m'b šlšn št w'nk mlkty 'ḥr 'by*. Both sentences in these lines are S + V + M.

[17] Other constructions have been characterized as "pluperfect" by scholars.

S. E. Loewenstamm noted an odd use of the active participle in Tannaitic Hebrew (*m. Šabb.* 10:1) and a construction borrowed from Aramaic into Amoraic Hebrew consisting of *hyh + passive participle* which marked the pluperfect ("The Pluperfect in Talmudic Hebrew," *From Babylon to Canaan* [Jerusalem: Magnes, 1992] 32–34; originally published in Hebrew in *Leš* 31 [1967] 21–22).

Neither of these usages was particularly productive. The almost total discontinuity between the structures of the verbal system in biblical and mishnaic Hebrew makes it highly unlikely that there is a connection between the features noted by Loewenstamm and the pluperfect construction in the earlier system.

M. Azar's authoritative study of mishnaic syntax on the basis of the excellent Kaufman manuscript does not refer to the past perfect at all (*The Syntax of Mishnaic Hebrew* [Hebrew; Jerusalem: The Academy of the Hebrew Language and University of Haifa, 1995]).

S. Segert recognizes a formal pluperfect construction in a third century BCE Phoenician formed by the perfect form of the verb "to be", *k-w-n* followed by the perfect of another verb: *hndr 'š kn ndr 'bnm*, "the vow which their father had vowed" *KAI* 40:5 (*A Grammar of Phoenician and Punic* [München: C. H. Beck, 1976] 192 *ad* §64.421.21). This is quite unlike the biblical Hebrew construction, but has an analogous parallel in Arabic. (Cf. the following note.) However, if *ndr* in the Phoenician text is a participle, it may supply an analogue for the construction identified by Loewenstamm.

Three examples are found in the Phoenician inscription of Kilamu, ca. 830–25 BCE (*KAI* 24:10–12):

> And I—to some I was a father and to some I was a mother and to some I was a brother, *wmy bl ḥz pn š*, and who had not seen the face of a lamb, I made him owner of a flock, *wmy bl ḥz pn 'lp*, and who had not seen the face of a bull, I made him owner of cattle..., *wmy bl ḥz ktn mn'ry*, and who had not seen a tunic since his youth, in my days linen covered him.[18]

M. S. Smith suggests that in the Ugaritic idiom *bph rgm lyṣ'a* (KTU 1.19 ii 26; iii 7, 35), the *qtl* has verb has pluperfect force, i.e., "from his mouth the message had not left..." ("The **qatala* Form in Ugaritic Narrative Poetry," *Pomegranates and Golden Bells: Studies in Biblical, Jewish, and Near Eastern Ritual, Law and Literature in Honor of Jacob Milgrom* [eds. D. P. Wright et al.; Winona Lake: Eisenbrauns, 1995] 794). This pluperfect translation is not the only possible one, though it is appropriate in context.

[18] Cf. J. Friedrich and W. Röllig, *Phönizisch-Punishce Grammatik* (Roma: Pontificium Institutum Biblicum, 1970) 132; Segert, *A Grammar of Phoenician and Punic*, 192, §64.421.2

Segert also notes "a formal plusquamperfect" marked, as in Arabic, by the verb "to be" in *KAI* 40:5, *hndr 'š kn ndr 'bnm*, "the oath which their father had vowed," a 3rd century BCE inscription from Idalion in Cyprus (cf. §64.421.21). This was also noted by E. König, *Syntax der hebräischen Sprache*, 43, §122, citing Th. Nöldeke.

In Arabic, the pluperfect is formally indicated by the confirmatory particle *qad* or the verb *kāna* followed by a *qatala* (W. Wright, *A Grammar of the Arabic Language*, vol. II (third edition; Cambridge: Cambridge University Press, 1964; [published originally, 1898]) 4–8; J. A. Haywood and H. M. Nahmad, *A New Arabic Grammar of the Written Language* (Cambridge: Harvard University Press, 1962) 100, 104–05).

Inasmuch as Segert's example is unique in the Phoenician-Punic corpus, another possible interpretation may be considered. The dedicatory inscription refers to statues being set up by Bath-shalom daughter of PN for three descendants of PN. Line 5 could be translated: "the oath was the oath of their father, PN during his life."

If, however, the Punic example is accepted as pluperfect, it indicates that the verbal system of Phoenician-Punic changed during the approximately 500 years between the Kilamu inscription and this one from Cyprus.

IV

BACKGROUNDING

Biblical narrators oriented their audiences to the world of their story by presenting information without which the story would make no sense. Although they presupposed audience knowledge about many things, including language, dress, manners and ethical codes, it was still necessary to provide some general information about characters, location, and time. So, the story of Judah and Tamar begins typically:

> And it was at that time (i.e., after the brothers sold Joseph in chapter 37—zz), and Judah went down from his brothers and pitched his tent by that of an Adullamite man, named Hiram; and Judah saw there the daughter of a Canaanite man named Shua.... (Gen 38:1)

Similarly, Gen 39:1 begins, "And Joseph was brought down to Egypt, and Potiphar, a courtier of Pharaoh, his chief steward bought him...." (Cf. also, Exod 1:1–8; 2:1; Josh 2:1; 6:1–2; Judg 3:15; 4:1–5; 6:11; 11:1; etc.) Not all expositional information had to be provided up front in so straightforward a manner.

Backgrounding refers to that part of literary composition concerned with fleshing out given events or characters, contextualizing them in time, place, and circumstances. The anterior construction, described in the previous chapter, was available for backgrounding of a particular type. An author could provide background, either through the words of characters or through his own narrative voice, by significant detail or allusion.[1] The anterior con-

---

[1] Backgrounding is akin to, but should not be confused with, characterization. For the latter, cf. Berlin, *Poetics and Interpretation*, 33–42; Sternberg, *Poetics of Biblical Narrative*, 322–41. For exposition in general, cf. Sternberg, *Expositional Modes and Temporal Ordering in Fiction* (Baltimore and London: Johns Hopkins University Press, 1978) 1–34.

struction was used with the second option as part of the creative doling out of information.[2]

Use of the anterior construction for backgrounding may be compared with the more common way of backgrounding through mention of a detail or an event that may not be relevant to its immediate context but whose importance becomes obvious only as the story unfolds, i.e., foreshadowing. In some cases, the background material is distant from that part of the narrative within which it becomes significant; in others, it immediately precedes it.

Examples of the former are the following: genealogical information in Gen 22:20–24 about Abraham's family back in Haran, reported after Isaac was not sacrificed on Mt. Moriah, backgrounds the match-making narrative of chapter 24; casual mention of the birth of Dinah after the list of Leah's sons in Gen 30:21 anticipates the complex story of her assignation in 34:1–31; the significance of the long-sleeved tunic made for Joseph by his father in Gen 37:3 clarifies its symbolic significance when the brothers strip it off from Joseph in 37:23; the prohibition to take spoils at Jericho mentioned in Josh 6:18–19 becomes significant only after Achan violates the ban in 7:1, 11; the reference to the "evil spirit" from YHWH that afflicts Saul in 1 Sam 16:14–16 backgrounds later stories in 18:10 and 19:9 that describe how the spirit influences actions; the mention that David deposited Goliath's armor in YHWH's tent in 1 Sam 17:54 backgrounds the Nob priest's offer of Goliath's sword to David in 21:10; the description of Absalom's locks in 2 Sam 14:25–26 backgrounds his hair raising demise in 2 Sam 18:9.

Examples of backgrounding that immediately precede the relevant disclosure moment in narrative are the description of Joseph's good looks in Gen 39:6b that anticipates Mrs. Potiphar's wandering eyes in 39:7; the oblique mention of Ehud's dexterity with his left hand in Judg 3:15 highlights the stratagem enabling Ehud to assassinate Eglon in 3:21; the specific mention that Eglon received Ehud in his upper chamber, possibly a toilet, in Judg 3:20 illuminates details of Ehud's escape in 3:23–26; reference to the season of wheat harvesting, an activity of the early summer when the stalks have dried out in Judg 15:1 explains how Samson's arson resulted in so much damage to

---

[2] This aspect of biblical narrative has not been treated monographically in any significant detail. F. Polak's summary treatment of some backgrounding elements has the advantage of being presented in a context of contemporary literary theory (*Biblical Narrative. Aspects of Art and Design* [Hebrew; Jerusalem: Mosad Bialik, 1994] 81–90, 155–74 and bibliography).

the Philistines in 15:5; the reference to Saul's extraordinary physical stature in 1 Sam 9:2 explains the excited half-sentences of the young women in 9:12 as well as YHWH's chastising statement to Samuel for presuming that a king had to be physically impressive in 1 Sam 16:6–7; the mention of Bathsheba's bathing and beauty in 2 Sam 11:2 that backgrounds David's attraction to her in 11:3–4a also establishes beyond doubt the paternity of the child in 11:4b–5.[3]

At first impression, the difference between anticipatory backgrounding and the postponed backgrounding of the anterior construction appears to be that the former is a mark of skilled literary craftsmanship while the latter indicates careless afterthought.[4] The latter may also be described more charitably and with greater precision as a form of internal commentary and clarification. Furthermore, close examination of the latter reveals an additional difference. Anticipatory backgrounding is self-contained, but the retrospective backgrounding of the examples presented above is often loose-ended and incomplete, hinting at the existence of more information than the narrator/author provided or wished to provide. This is because many of the clauses presuppose authorial knowledge of comprehensive stories or events from which only some pertinent pieces of information were plucked. Some examples presented in chapter III are actually adjacent to either fuller narratives or supplementary information: Gen 6:7–8, cf. verses 9–10; Num 13:30–31, cf. Num 14:2; Judg 3:25–26, cf. verses 22–23. It is noteworthy that according to various formulations of the documentary hypothesis the supple-

---

[3] Y. Zakovitch provides a descriptive taxonomy of the different narrative functions of anticipatory backgrounding ("Foreshadowing in Biblical Narrative," *Beer-Sheva* 2 [1985] 104–05 [Hebrew]).

[4] As the term itself indicates, "afterthought" in speech, and often in writing, designates the correction of an earlier omission. This understanding clarifies it at the surface level of the final communication. However, at an even deeper level, it is now becoming clear to neurobiologists that the hippocampus, at the lower rear of the brain, tags and sequences sensorial data preserving them in a serial order, possibly in degrees of "pastness." Thus, the organization of events in chronological sequence, in time, is not an abstract concept but a neurophysiological fact expressed linguistically. If only for this reason, it should be considered a primal feature in languages (cf. R. W. Doty, "Time and Memory," *Brain Organization and Memory* [eds. J. L. McGaugh, N. Weinberger, G. Lynch; New York and Oxford: Oxford University Press, 1990] 148–51, 154). Consequently, what appears as "afterthought" in the final communication of a biblical narrative may sometimes be a correction for chronological slippage or, if planned, it may be a creative torquing of time. M. H. Gottstein suggested that it be studied as a phenomenon of what he termed "abnormal syntax" ("Afterthought and the Syntax of Relative Clauses in Biblical Hebrew," *JBL* 68 [1949] 38).

mentary information associated with Gen 6:7–8 and Num 13:30–31 is associated with a source different from that containing the backgrounding: Gen 6:7–8 = JE; Gen 6:9–10 = P; Num 13:30–31 = JE; Num 14:2 = P. These, however, are the exceptions.

More common are those cases where authors revealed less rather than more information. For example, Gen 2:25–3:1 presupposes a narrative about the formation of various creatures and the determination of their nature; Judg 10:18–11:1 presupposes a repertoire of hero stories; 1 Sam 28:2–3 presupposes a full narrative about the death of Samuel that told how he was mourned throughout Israel; 2 Sam 18:18 presupposes more information about the construction of Absalom's memorial that may have explained what happened to his three sons (cf. 2 Sam 14:27); 2 Kgs 3:4 presupposes additional knowledge about the early career of Mesha and his wars with Israel, some details of which are known from the Moabite stone; 2 Kgs 17:29–34 assumes additional knowledge about the backgrounds and cultic practices of Babylonians, Kuthians, and Hamatians. Although each anterior clause in these verses is self-contained syntactically, it is not independent narratively.

Recognition of this syntactic structure and of its meaning has significance for literary analysis. For example, if not noted in Gen 34:6–7, v. 7 could be taken as indicating that only after Hamor came to talk with him did Jacob send for his sons.[5] This flat, sequential reading is not warranted on grammatical grounds. Actually, the narrative in vv. 6–7 indicates that the sons of Jacob had come from the field saddened and angry after they had they heard about Dinah and Shechem:

> And Hamor, father of Shechem went to Jacob to speak with him, *wbny y'qb b'w*, but the sons of Jacob had come from the field when they heard; and the men were saddened and it angered them greatly. (Gen 34:6–7a)

So, when Hamor and Shechem arrived at Jacob's house the brothers were already there—silent, sullen, and seething. The story presupposes that in their discussion with Hamor and Shechem the brothers' duplicity was apparent neither to the foreigners nor to their own father. Their plan succeeded because,

---

[5] Fruchtman, "A Few Notes," 65. Her article deals primarily with circumstantial participial clauses, topic sentences, and what she deemed the pluperfect construction (pp. 64–66). Fruchtman develops the theme that attention to grammatical, especially syntactic, subtleties restricts the number of potential "readings" and interpretations that literary analysis can suggest, whereas inattention to them may result in readings that are demonstrably incorrect.

after experiencing and expressing their anger in the field, they suppressed and masked it when meeting potential in-laws at their father's home.

Similarly, recognizing the anterior construction clarifies that what otherwise might be considered an out-of-sequence piece of narrative is actually due to a grammatical device employed artistically (cf. Gen 2:25–3:1; 7:18–19; 15:17; Exod 33:6–7; Num 5:13–14; 13:30–31).

V

THE TENSE/ASPECT PROBLEM

In the fourth paragraph of chapter III above, I suggested that the distinction between pluperfect and preperfect is useful in part because preperfect examples are not always rendered easily into English, but did not elaborate. The following discussion will help clarify why this is so.

In Hebrew, as in other languages, verbs may be distinguished according to the inherent semantic features that they express. Some are "telic," referring to an activity with a discernible moment of culmination, e.g., *mṣ'*, "he found," (Gen 6:7–8); *yldh*, "she bore," (Gen 16:1); *pqd*, "he took account of," (Gen 20:18–21:1); *šlḥh*, "she sent" (Gen 38:24b–25). Among these cited examples, two may also be characterized as "punctual," expressing an action concluded in a relatively short period of time, *yldh* and *pqd*. Other verbs express durative, habitual, stative, and indeterminate activities, e.g., *h-y-h* (Gen 4:2; 11:2); *b-w-'* (Gen 4:3–4; 19:23–24; 27:30; 41:56–57); *hwṣy'*, "he brought out," (Gen 14:17–18); *hlk*, "he went," (Gen 26:25–26; 32:1–2).

Such classification according to the type and quality of action, *Aktionsart*, expressed by a verb in context clarifies why most passages were filed under the "pluperfect" or "preperfect" rubrics in chapter III and usually eliminates the necessity of explaining this filing in terms of translation equivalents. Verbs expressing telicity and punctuality were usually classified as "pluperfect." Those not expressing telicity and those expressing it but lacking a well defined sense of punctuality were classified as "preperfect."

There are, however, some exceptions among the examples listed in chapter III, e.g., *h-y-h* bears a pluperfect sense in Gen 15:17 and Num 27:3 while *hmṭyr* has a preperfect sense in Gen 19:23–24 as does *ns'* in Gen 33:16–17. These suggest that at a high theoretical level the *Aktionsart* of all relevant verbs, those in the main line narrative as well as that in the anterior construction, are best considered in tandem. Together they create context, describing and delimiting the dynamic quality of states and activities. Thus, hard focusing on the verb in the anterior construction may be ill advised.

Considered at a less theoretical level, the exceptions point to the possibility that translation may still be a factor to be dealt with, since the semantics of the translation verbs in target languages may differ from those of the source word in Hebrew and thus mislead. This topic cannot be addressed until semanticists describe and map the varieties of *Aktionsart* in Hebrew.[1]

Grammatically, the descriptive categories pluperfect and preperfect used above are irrelevant since they address a semantic matter bearing on when the action or state described by a verb concluded. The anterior construction in and of itself, however, indicates only that the activity of the verb commenced prior to that of the past tense verb in the preceding clause. At the syntactic-semantic level of analysis, then, **the anterior construction engages the Hebrew verbal system only insofar as that system indicates tense, not aspect.** Therefore, the analysis presented above can be correct only if the Hebrew verbal system was a tensed and not an aspectual one.

This statement is buttressed by observations made on the basis of world languages considered typologically. J. L. Bybee notes that "anterior does not occur in languages that do not have other tense distinctions marked inflectionally."[2] Biblical Hebrew, however, is not considered a tensed language by many.

---

[1] Two studies provide complementary approaches to achieve this mapping. C. Bache describes types of characteristics assigned to verbs expressing actions. He classifies these in hierarchical categories and claims that they have universal application (*The Study of Aspect, Tense and Action. Towards a Theory of the Semantics of Grammatical Categories* [Frankfurt am Main: Peter Lang, 1995] 236–54, 313–15). Although Bache's analysis is based entirely on English, it does not appear to be language specific and should be translatable to classical Hebrew.

C. L. Tenny proposes a disciplined approach to achieve this mapping using a broader spread of categories than Bache that appears adaptable for biblical Hebrew ("Lexical Conceptual Structures and Aspectual Roles," *Aspectual Rules and the Syntax-Semantics Interface* [Studies in Linguistics and Philosophy 52; Dordrecht: Kluwer Academic Publishers, 1994] 182–220). Cf. also the earlier suggestions of B. Comrie, *Aspect: An Introduction to the Study of Verbal Aspect and Related Problems* (Cambridge: Cambridge University Press, 1976) 130–32.

[2] J. L. Bybee, *Morphology. A Study of the Relationship Between Meaning and Form* (Amsterdam: John Benjamin's Publishing, 1985) 160. For examples of what she calls "anteriority" corresponding to pluperfect and preperfect, cf. pp. 159–62. Cf. also, B. Comrie, *Tense* (Cambridge: Cambridge University Press, 1985) 125–27.

Major reference grammars as well as commonly used textbooks of biblical Hebrew describe the verbal system as one indicating aspects, not tenses. These grammars do allow that verbs in the perfect aspect usually refer to past happenings that are, *ipso facto*, usually concluded, while those in the imperfect aspect usually refer to happenings in the present or future that are incomplete. In view of the obvious contradiction between my statement about the implications of the anterior construction and the common comprehension of the Hebrew verbal system, the issue is taken up now.

Tense systems have to do with time; aspect systems have to do with duration. Tense systems indicate when an act or event took place in time along a chronological axis. The writer/speaker refers to or presupposes one event as the fixed, benchmark event (cf. various uses of expressions referring to "this day," Gen 19:37–38; 22:14; 2 Kgs 17:23, 34, 41; etc.), and indicates whether other events occurred before, simultaneously with, or after the fixed event. In biblical narrative, the time of the writer is the fixed event, so that the narrative refers to past happenings. However, within the narrative time frame imposed by the writer, different characters may use other fixed events as benchmarks. They may refer to present or future events using appropriate verbs, events which are all past from the author's perspective, e.g., Exod 3:3a: *wy'mr*, And Moses thought/said, *'srh-n' w'r'h*, I will indeed turn and I will see this great sight. The verb *wy'mr* reflects the writer's fixed event; the verbs *'srh-n' w'r'h* bespeak Moses' fixed event as the moment of his comprehending the uniqueness of the burning bush and his determination to do some things in his future after the moment of understanding.[3] Everything described was a past event from the author's benchmark, but some were present-future from the perspective of Moses.

Aspect—derived from Latin, *aspicere*, "to look at"— refers to the internal quality of an act while it occurs, its relative duration during the time of the event as represented from the point of view of the author or character. The act may be expressed as perfective, i.e., completed, or imperfective, i.e., incomplete or in process, as habitual, progressive, repeated, or intensive. Theoretically, the distinctions made by aspect are independent of when the act occurs. In actuality, different languages handle aspect differently, depending

---

[3] Cf. J. E. Clifford, *Tense and Tense Logic* (The Hague: Mouton, 1975) 29–33; Sauer, *A Formal Semantics of Tense, Aspect, and Aktionsart* (Bloomington, IN: Indiana University Linguistics Club, 1984) 35–39; Comrie, *Aspect*, 26–40.

on their analytic principles, linguistic resources, and grammatical structures. So, what is attested in one may not be assumed automatically to be present in even a closely related language, or if present, to function in the same way or to make the same types of distinctions.[4]

In Russian, and in other Slavic languages, verb stems are augmented in various ways marking them both for aspect and for tense. Thus, instantaneous or complete or single acts are marked perfective and can be represented either as taking place in the past or future;[5] repeated or durative acts can be represented as taking place in the past, present, or future.[6] Grammarians of Slavic languages introduced the term "aspect" into linguistic parlance.

A good case can be made that the English verbal system also indicates both tense and aspect. Consider the following:

> Abraham walks. (simple present)
>> Abraham has walked. (present perfect)
> Abraham walked. (simple past)
>> Abraham had walked. (past perfect)
> Abraham will walk. (simple future)
>> Abraham will have walked. (future perfect)

In these, the contrast between sets is obvious. Sentences in each set, e.g., simple present and present perfect, convey essentially the same information about the same person doing the same thing at the same time. The difference between them lies only in the duration of the act. It is represented by the perfect as complete whether occurring in the past, present, or future, while the act represented by the simple tenses is indefinite and incomplete whether occurring in the past, present, or future. Consequently, it could be concluded

---

[4] W. H. Hirtle, *Time, Aspect and the Verb* (Quebec: Les Presses de L'université Laval, 1975) 22–23. For informative examples, cf. the comparative study of world languages selected from major language families by Ö. Dahl, *Tense and Aspect Systems* (Oxford: Basil Blackwell, 1985).

[5] In Russian, the perfective also denotes that the results of the action are achieved, and therefore, it has no present tense since the results of an act occurring in present time cannot be achieved in the present. Only the imperfective verbs occur in a true present tense (H. G. Lunt, *Fundamentals of Russian* [The Hague: Mouton, 1954] 60–61).

[6] N. Forbes, *Russian Grammar* (third edition; Oxford: Clarendon Press, 1964) 267–85; Comrie, *Aspect*, 14, 71, 88–94; R. I. Binnick, *Time and the Verb. A Guide to Tense and Aspect* (New York: Oxford University Press, 1991) 135–39.

that tenses in English represent time while the aspect of completed activity is marked in each tense by the perfect. Incomplete acts, i.e., imperfect ones, are not marked *per se*; alternatively, they may be described as marked by "Ø," the absence of any modification or supplementation to the base form of the verb.

In actual use, however, English past and future perfect are rarely used independently of a benchmark time to which they mark anteriority or posteriority. Sentences of the type "Abraham will have offered Isaac" are not attested without explicit or implicit reference to a tensed verb, e.g., "Abraham will have offered Isaac before the sun will set." The following, although poorly formed, is possible: "Abraham will have offered Isaac before the sun will have set." The time reference role of the adverbial prepositional phrase in these sentences is crucial since the following sentence makes little sense: "Abraham will have offered Isaac after the sun will set."

The situation in English, then, is different from Russian.[7] Aspectual distinctions may be expressed in the present and, under certain circumstances, in the future. With regard to the past, the past perfect does not mark any aspect; it indicates only the past to the past. There is no difference in meaning between "Joseph presented his sons and Jacob blessed them" and "Joseph had presented his sons and Jacob blessed them." It is clear in both sentences that the presenting, for as long as it may have taken, preceded and was concluded before the blessing commenced (cf. "The room was pitch dark; Max had switched off the light"). With regard to aspect, then, the first sentence of this paragraph may be rewritten: The system in English is radically different both from that of Russian as well as from that commonly assumed for Hebrew.

Linguists consider some languages to be tenseless, e.g., Bantu languages, Burmese, and Chinese.[8] This does not imply that users of these languages fail to note linear time or that they cannot indicate that the cows milked yesterday will have to be milked tomorrow. It does imply, however, that information bearing on linear time is not grammaticized in the language, i.e., it is not ex-

---

[7] The English perfect is not equivalent to the perfective in Russian. For the complexity of the Russian system through the prism of a French linguist, cf. R. Valin, "The Aspects of the French Verb," translated in Hirtle, *Time, Aspect, and the Verb*, 132–35. Valin concludes that French too indicates both tense and aspect. On aspect in English, cf. Forbes, *Russian Grammar*, 268. Sauer discusses the English system in detail (*A Formal Semantics*, 35–36, 69–77) while C. S. Smith provides a more up to date analysis (*The Parameters of Aspect* [Studies in Linguistics and Philosophy 43; Dordrecht: Kluwer Academic Publishers, 1991] 253–95).

[8] Comrie, *Tense*, 50; Comrie, *Aspect*, 81–82, 94; Smith, *The Parameter of Aspect*, 343.

pressed through special verbal forms. In tenseless languages, aspectual information is grammaticized while information bearing on linear time is lexicalized, i.e., expressed through the use of special particles or dedicated words.[9] An example of lexicalization is English "have," which sometimes loses its semantic content of "to grasp, seize" and marks perfectivity, e.g., "I have done it," as well as indicating obligation, e.g., "I have to go," and possession, e.g., "I have a book."[10]

The theoretical inverse of a tenseless language would be an aspectless one in which tense is grammaticized and aspect lexicalized. To the best of my knowledge, no such language is known, so the example of Chinese as tenseless lacks a true polar opposite.

The discussion to this point suffices for the following three observations: 1) Languages with grammaticized aspect have lexicalized tense systems; some also have a partially grammaticized tense system. 2) Tensed languages may also have grammaticized aspect systems or lexicalized ones. 3) With regard to its quantitative and qualitative presentation of tense and aspect through lexicalization and grammaticization, any natural language lies on a continuum between tenseless Mandarin Chinese and its theoretical inverse, an aspectless language.[11] These, in turn, have profound implications for Hebrew grammar

---

[9] Comrie, *Tense*, 9–10; Comrie, *Aspect*, 5–6; B. Heine, U. Claudi, F. Hünnemeyer, *Grammaticization. A Conceptual Framework* (Chicago: University of Chicago Press, 1991) 1–26.

[10] Heine et al., *Grammaticization*, 7.

[11] Cf. Ö. Dahl, *Tense and Aspect Systems*, 124–28. Dahl's comparative study indicates that many aspect languages also have a future tense. (I ignore Dahl's classifications of Hebrew and Arabic which are based on conventional grammars.)

In his major study of various descriptions of the verbal system in the Bible, L. McFall, refers off-handedly to "tenseless languages," (*The Enigma of the Hebrew Verbal System* [Sheffield: Almond Press, 1982] 20). The accompanying footnote on p. 220 refers to some West African languages such as Yoruba and Igbo that do not distinguish between past and present, and in which non-stative verbs are marked if they have an imperfective meaning. He cites W. E. Welmers, *African Language Structures* (Berkeley: University of California Press, 1973) 345–47.

On the basis of the information cited above from McFall, we could conclude that these languages distinguish between future and non-future (= past-present) in the verbal system, and that within the system, verbs which are stative and incomplete with regard to their *Aktionsart* are never marked, while verbs that are active and transitive with regard to their *Aktionsart* are marked when imperfective.

Welmers' analysis itself is not readily applicable to this discussion of Hebrew because he employs the term "verbal constructions" rather than "system" as a way of emphasizing the

because, as mentioned earlier in this chapter, descriptions of Hebrew since the middle of the 19th century have presented the Hebrew verb as lacking tenses.

This way of describing the verbal system became popular through the later editions of G. H. A. von Ewald's *Kritische Grammatik der hebräischen Sprache*.[12] In the second edition of 1835, Ewald introduced the Latin terms *perfectum* and *imperfectum* to describe what was expressed by the *qatal* and *yiqtol* forms of conjugated verbs respectively. The former was used to refer to completed actions, the latter to actions yet incomplete.[13] This edition was translated into English in 1836, and thus the idea and terminology entered Anglo-American discussions.

---

difference between the European grammars and those of the African languages; and he also coins new terminology to describe various unique features (pp. 310, 315). However, a grammar of Yoruba written by a native speaker using the conventional terms "tense and aspect" indicates that both are to be found, partly grammaticized and partly lexicalized (cf. P. O. Ogunbowale, *The Essentials of the Yoruba Language* [London: University of London Press, 1970] 49–63).

In Igbo, the system appears to be more complex, with formal elements indicting aspect more developed. Nevertheless, as in Yoruba, time is indicated by certain constructions (B. F. Welmers and W. E. Welmers, *Igbo: A Learner's Manual* [Los Angeles: Dept. of Linguistics, UCLA, 1968] 75–76, 85, 87).

Despite the non-traditional terminology coined to describe the languages, Welmers' work in his study of structures and in his teaching grammar indicates that both chronological as well as durational distinctions are made in these languages.

[12] The grammar, published in Leipzig, went through four editions: 1827, 1835, 1838, 1844.

[13] V. DeCaen, "Ewald and Driver on Biblical Hebrew 'Aspect': Anteriority and the Orientalist Framework," *ZAH* 9 (1996) 134–38.

DeCaen points out that Ewald himself did not use the term aspect or a German equivalent *Zeitart* and argues that he viewed the system as marking sequentiality rather than aspect proper. DeCaen proposes that it was S. R. Driver who first explained the system as aspectual but that C. Brockelman was actually the first to employ the term in 1951 (pp. 137–47). Although he may be correct, the oblique and implicit evidence adduced to demonstrate that Ewald was not (or could not have been) thinking about aspect is far from clear.

The seventeenth edition of Gesenius' grammar published in 1856 contains the following note: "It is a false view which regards the so-called Perfect and Imperfect not as tenses, but as designed originally to express distinctions of mood rather than relations of time" (T. J. Conant, *Gesenius' Hebrew Grammar: Seventeenth Edition, With Numerous Corrections and Additions, by Dr. E. Rödiger* [New York: D. Appleton & Co., 1856] 223.) The "false view" against which Rödiger protested, appears to have been something approaching aspect.

Ewald's work on Hebrew and then on Arabic (1831–33) reflect the influence of information about aspect in Slavic languages that entered western European grammatical discourse in the early nineteenth century. By the early nineteenth century, "aspect" explanations had been applied both to modern and ancient non-Slavic languages, e.g., Greek, Latin, and German. It was only a matter of time until the notion was applied to Semitic languages.

Prior to Ewald, scholars worked with some concept of tense to describe the Hebrew system, and even after Ewald's ideas became widespread, some still continued to do so.[14] However, the influence of S. R. Driver, who applied the notion of "aspect" in his description and explanation of the workings of the Hebrew verbal system at the end of the nineteenth century, and the quasi-canonical status of 20th century versions of *Gesenius' Hebrew Grammar* in various translations that accepted Driver's analysis won the day for the aspect hypothesis. Canonicity, however, is no guarantor of correctness.[15]

In the terminology introduced above, most contemporary descriptions characterize the Hebrew verbal system as grammaticizing the perfect and imperfect aspects but lacking any distinctive grammaticized or lexicalized way to indicate linear time. They thus imply that Hebrew is unique and that it does

---

[14] For example, I. Nordheimer referred to the "preterite and future tenses" of indicative verbs in his *A Critical Grammar of the Hebrew Language* (second edition; New York: Wiley and Putnam, 1842) 108–09, §155.

[15] McFall, *The Enigma*, 43–57, 184–85; Binnick, *Time and the Verb*, pp. 139–42, 435; cf. DeCaen, "Ewald and Driver," 143–44.

A recent application of the aspect hypothesis to literary texts is that of M. Eskhult, *Studies in Verbal Aspect and Narrative Technique in Biblical Hebrew Prose* (Uppsala: Almqvist & Wiksell International, 1990). Eskhult notes the *we PN qatal* construction, considering it as indicating a "state" or "a being so and so" that functions as a device to mark the beginning of a new episode (pp. 55, 57).

Many of the examples that he cites to illustrate his point are from the Elisha stories, which are not a continuous narrative but a collage comprised of a series of unconnected or minimally connected anecdotes edited by the cut and paste method (e.g., 2 Kgs 4:1; 4:38; 4:42; 5:1–2; 6:8; 8:1). Thus they fail to meet one criterion for anterior constructions, that of coming after a verb in the past, because the preceding verb is part of an unrelated anecdote. Note, however, that the construction is attested within a few of these narratives and are listed above, e.g., 2 Kgs 8:29b; 9:1.

Eskhult's examples indicate that the anterior construction developed from or is a special application of a device originally marking the introduction of a new subject/topic in a sequential order that was loosely linked via the common conjunction *waw* to an earlier subject/topic.

not correspond to any known natural language.[16] Such descriptions, actually hypotheses about the system, lack empirical corroboration and often justify themselves self-referentially through translation—a topic addressed in chapter II above. Finally, they fail to clarify why these "aspects" function most of the time like well defined tenses.[17] In the light of contemporary linguistic knowledge and descriptive terminology, they are inadequate hypotheses.[18]

Any attempt to translate the six sentences used above to illustrate the tense-aspect system of English into classical Hebrew will result in failure to find verbal semantic equivalents for the perfects, hesitation on how to render the present, the use of *hālak* for the simple past, and of *yēlēk* for the simple future. This is because the verbal system of classical Hebrew, Hebrew of Iron

---

[16] A comparison of Hebrew with the Mandarin system as described by Smith is highly instructive (*The Parameter of Aspect*, 343–90). Granting for the sake of this note that Hebrew is tenseless, its lack of devices for marking time is astounding.

[17] In this discussion, I address "aspect" in the most general way purposely and do not seek to distinguish among terms such as perfective, habitual, and durative. The latter two terms are sometimes used synonymously but may be distinguished since in a given language verbs with one type of *Aktionsart* may function differently with regard to tense than verbs with a different type. Little work, if any, has been done on this topic in Hebrew, so that not enough is known to justify being overly specific. Cf. Bache, *The Study of Aspect*, 268–69; Tenny, *Aspectual Rules*, 182–220; Ö. Dahl, "Perfectivity in Slavic and other languages," *Aspect Bound: A Voyage into the realm of Germanic, Slavonic, and Finno-Ugrian aspectology* (eds. C. de Groot and H. Tommola; Dordrecht: Foris Publications and USA: Cinnaminson, 1984) 1–6, 18. The work of both Tenny and Dahl is suggestive for what may be attempted in Hebrew.

[18] There are of course exceptions. T. Muraoka is one of the first contemporary grammarians to express his discomforture with prevailing descriptions of the Hebrew verb in a grammar that is gaining an increasing readership. He opts for the terms "perfect" and "future," and although sensitive to the issues that the term "aspect" is said to have resolved, treats the system as tensed (Joüon-Muraoka, *A Grammar of Biblical Hebrew*, 354–57, §111).

In 1974, W. Schneider reached similar conclusions. He approached the verbal system from a text-grammar perspective. Schneider considered it tensed but functioning differently when used in the narrative framework (*Erzählen*) and in human discourse (*Besprechen*) (*Grammatik des Biblischen Hebräisch* [München: Claudius, 1993; first printed, 1974] 182–208). Schneider, whose approach, like that adopted here, was formal, also distinguished between how tenses are used in the texts and how they are conventionally rendered in German (p. 208). Cf. the important review and extension of this work by E. Talstra in *BO* 35 (1979) 169–74; 39 (1982) 26–38. (I thank Dr. F. Polack for bringing both Schneider's book and Talstra's reviews to my attention.)

In addition to the abovementioned scholars, it is my impression that many contemporary Israeli scholars now assume that biblical Hebrew was essentially a tensed language—different from both mishnaic and modern Hebrew. Cf. Rubinstein, *Contemporary Hebrew and Ancient Hebrew*, 14–19 and Blau, *A Grammar*, 45–46.

Age II (ca. 1000–586 BCE), did not develop a panoply of subtly differentiated aspectual nuances. In Hebrew, tense was grammaticized while aspect was indicated in a variety ways.[19]

---

[19] There is no reason that "dead" languages which were once "living" should fall into a special category. Tenses are quite obvious in Phoenician, Moabite, Ammonite, Syriac, and Arabic.

In prose, the Ugaritic verbal system functions like its Hebrew counterpart and has no "aspectual" surprises. On the use of verbs in Ugaritic, cf. S. Segert, *A Basic Grammar of the Ugaritic Language* (Berkeley: University of California Press, 1984) 56, who refers to aspects but notes that the function of the forms is temporal. On pp. 89–90, Segert describes the verbal system in prose as tensed but in poetry as aspectual. Contrast J. Blau who speaks of Ugaritic poetic grammar as tensed ("Marginalia Semtica III," *IOS* 7 [1977] 23–27). A. Rainey ("A New Grammar of Ugaritic," *Or* 56 [1988] 397–99) and D. Sivan (*Ugaritic Grammar* [Hebrew; Jerusalem: Bialik Institute, 1993] 63–71) treat the verbal system as tensed; and cf. T. L. Fenton, "The Hebrew 'Tenses' in the Light of Ugaritic," *Proceedings of the Fifth World Congress of Jewish Studies*, vol. 4 (1969) 31–39.

In 1975, S. Segert addressed problems with the use of aspect to describe the Semitic verbal system. His solution was to modify and slightly redefine the traditional terminology rather than to jettison it as an incorrect, misleading encumbrance ("Verbal Categories of Some Northwest Semitic Languages: A Didactic Approach," *Afroasiatic Linguistics* 2:5 [1975] 89–91).

VI

OVERLY TENSED:
THE FOUR FORMS OF THE TWO TENSES

Verbs in biblical Hebrew are marked by the use of prefixes, suffixes, and accent for past by the *qatál*-suffixed forms, and for present-future (= not past) by the *yiqtól*-prefixed forms. They are also marked for past by [*way*] *yíqtol*, and for present-future by [*we*] *qatál*.[1] The employment of *yiqtol* to narrate past events is attested also in Moabite where it occurs with and without a preceding conjunction: *w''š*, "and I made" (*KAI* 181:3); *wy'nw*, "and they afflicted/humbled" (*KAI* 181:5); *y'np*, "he was angry"(*KAI* 181:5); in Phoenician both in the Kilamu inscription: *ytlnn*, "they complained" (*KAI* 24:9); and in the Azitawadda inscription: *yšt'*, "he feared" (*KAI* 26:A II:4); in Aramaic in the Hamath inscription of Zakkur: *w'š'...wy'nny*, "and I lifted (my hands)...and he answered me" (*KAI* 202:A, 11); *wy'mr*, "and he said" (*KAI* 202:A, 15); and on a stele from Tel Dan: *ysq*, "he went up" (l. 2); *wyškb*, "and he lay (on his death bed)" (l. 3); *yhk*, "he went" (l. 3); *wy'l*, "they ascended" (l. 3); *wyhk*, "and he went" (l. 5); *w'qtl*, "and I killed" (l. 6); *w'šm*, "and I placed" (l. 9).[2] In addition to these, two restored forms are

---

[1] In both of these latter cases, I indicate the conditioned allomorphs of the conjunctive *waw* because that is how the verbal forms commonly appear in narrative prose for reasons adumbrated in chapter I.

The allomorph *waw* with the /a/ vowel is an archaic form of the conjunction in a fixed, stereotypical usage. Such "fixed word-combinations" remain in linguistic use even after other parts of the language have changed. Cf. Fenton, "Hebrew 'Tenses'," 32.

[2] J. Tropper, "Paläographische und linguistische Anmerkungen zur Steleninschrift aus Dan," *UF* 24 (1994) 489–91. T. Muraoka, "Linguistic Notes on the Aramaic Inscription from Tel Dan," *IEJ* 45 (1995) 19–20. Muraoka spells out the implications of these forms for other similar forms in Aramaic. (Despite the printed date of publication, Tropper cites Muraoka.) *wy'l* in l. 3 was discovered on a fragment of the inscription published after Muraoka's article

posited for a second fragment of the Dan inscription on the basis of context and syntax: [*w*]*yhmlk*, "and he made king" (B:4); [*w*]*'pq*, "and I departed" (B:6).[3]

Yiqtol forms narrating past events are attested also in Hebrew inscriptions: the Siloam inscription: *wylkw*, "and they flowed" (*KAI* 189:4); the Yavneh Yam ostracon: *wyqṣr*, "and he harvested" (*KAI* 200:4); and *wyb'...wyqḥ...*, "and he came and he took" (*KAI* 200:7–8); Lachish letters: *wy'lhw*, "and he took him up" (*KAI* 194:7). These extra-biblical data range chronologically from the eighth through the sixth centuries BCE.

In Hebrew, the original differentiator between a *yqtl* form indicating past and one indicating present-future time was the accent. Whereas *yiqtol* past was accented on the first syllable, *yiqtol* present-future was accented on the last: *yíq-tol* (< *yáq-tul*) versus *yiq-tól* (< *yaqtál^{u/a}*).[4]

The most obvious evidence for this differentiator is the correlation between the unambiguous time references to past or present-future on the one hand, and between specific morphological forms of verbs with "weak" consonants in the second or third root position in *Qal* and all verbs in *Hiphil* on the other. Verbs indicating the past employ the so-called "short form" of the verb while those indicating the present-future use the long ones. The accent of the former is indicated by the masoretic tone markers on the first syllable and of the latter on the last. Although masoretic notations are neither fool-proof nor entirely consistent for reasons that I suggest below—cf. *yāšíyr*, "he sang/recited" (Exod 15:1; Num 21:17); *yāsíyr*, "he removed" (Exod 34:34); *yābdíyl*, "he divided" (Deut 4:41); but note *yaqhél*, "he gathered together"

---

was written. Cf. A. Biran and J. Naveh, "The Tel Dan Inscription: A New Fragment," *IEJ* 45 (1995) 9.

In a second article responding to Tropper, Muraoka notes that the Aramaic forms with a *waw* do not indicate any evolution into a unique syntagm with its own phonetic shape like Hebrew *waw conversum* ("The Tel Dan Inscription and Aramaic/Hebrew Tenses," *Abr-Nahrain* 33 [1995] 113–15). His caution on this account is well advised. The evidence is inadequate for reaching a conclusion about this issue. Cf. the preceding note.

[3] Biran and Naveh, "The Tel Dan Inscription: A New Fragment," 12.

[4] Derivation of these forms from Late Bronze Canaanite is not the concern of this study. It is, however, apparent from both comparative data and historical reconstruction that at an earlier stage of the language their distinctiveness was more obvious. Cf. A. Rainey, "The Ancient Hebrew Prefix Conjugation in the Light of Amarnah Canaanite," *HS* 27 (1986) 4–19. Rainey's article served as the basis for a symposium on the history and semantics of the prefix conjugation published in *HS* 29 (1988).

In view of these new lines of research into the problem of "origins," the derivation of the thematic /o/ vowel in Hebrew *yíqtol* verbs remains open.

(1 Kgs 8:1), with the "short form" but the accent on the final syllable—they do conserve and transmit a liturgical reading tradition that froze prior to a partial shift in accent towards the first syllable of words. The shift is attested in the Hebrew of the Dead Sea Scrolls but is more characteristic of later Tannaitic Hebrew.[5]

The hypothesis concerning the role of accent in marking this distinction does not depend on masoretic notations exclusively. It is proposed with greater certainty upon consideration of three factors:

1) Homographic heteronyms with significantly different meanings that could occur in similar syntactic contexts must have been differentiated in natural speech situations. This circumstance sets up the theoretical desirability for a phonemic accent hypothesis since the hypothesis explains parsimoniously how Hebrew tethered the time referent to verbs of otherwise identical morphological shape.

English speakers are familiar with the notion underlying this hypothesis since accent functions similarly as a differentiator in parts of the English vocabulary. Cf. words such as cónvert (noun)/convért (verb); pérvert (noun)/pervért (verb); présent (noun)/presént (verb); désert (noun)/desért (verb); bláck bírd (a bird colored black)/blàckbírd (a specific type of bird).

2) The abovementioned differences in the orthography of certain verbal classes in *Qal* and of all verbs in *Hiphil* are clarified in part as deriving from forms with different accents—a situation preserved partially in the masoretic notations.

3) The observation that pronominally suffixed energic forms are added only to verbs indicating present-future time, i.e., *yiqtól* forms, is explained only through recourse to reconstruction involving the unique placement of accent in these forms.[6]

---

[5] Y. Kutscher, *The Language and Linguistic Background of the Isaiah Scroll (1 Q Isaᵃ)* (Leiden: E. J. Brill, 1974) 332–36; E. Qimron, *The Hebrew of the Dead Sea Scrolls* (Atlanta: Scholars Press, 1986) 40–42. This shift is reflected also in contemporary "Ashkenazic" Hebrew that may be traced back to Tiberian Hebrew of the seventh century CE via scholars who studied in Tiberias and then found their way to the Rhine Valley where they established academies.

[6] J. Blau, "Pronominal Third Person Singular Suffixes With and Without N in Biblical Hebrew," ErIsr 14 (1978) 125–31 (Hebrew); Rainey, "The Ancient Hebrew Prefix Conjugation," 10–11.
   Two exceptions are Judg 15:2, *w'tnnh*, and (so) I gave her, and 2 Kgs 9:33, *wyrmsnh*, and he trampled her (cf. E. J. Revell, "The System of the Verb in Standard Biblical Prose,"

One additional consideration may be proposed. The hypothesis that a phonemic accent distinguished verbs indicating past from those indicating present-future time in Hebrew explains the same phenomenon in contemporaneous Moabite, Phoenician, and Aramaic.[7] This consideration applies factors 1) and 2) above to a broad dialect area as well as across language boundaries in the case of Aramaic.[8] Examples from these languages suggest that the distinction must have developed at the latest in Canaanite dialects of the Late Bronze Age (ca. 1400–1200 BCE), that is, it existed already in proto-Hebrew or proto-Northwest Semitic.[9] The presence of phonemic stress in the verb system of two Aramaic dialects may be explained provisionally according to the wave theory of linguistic diffusion. A linguistic feature in Phoenician and Hebrew spread to regionally adjacent dialects of Aramaic.

This hypothesis provides *a priori* grounds for arguing that accent was similarly phonemic in distinguishing between different time references of *qatal* verbs. The argument is supported by the placement of masoretic tone markings on accented syllables distinguishing between *qatal* past and *qatal* present-future in the 1st and 2nd person singular.

The formally marked difference between *qatál-ti/ta* past and *qatal-tí/tá* present-future provides *a posteriori* grounds for the argument, demonstrating the validity of the phonemic accent hypothesis for 1 sg. and 2 sg. in the regular paradigm while providing support for the more general hypothesis. This is not an original observation. In one form or another, it has been maintained by most scholars since it was suggested in 1550 by Elias Levita, who considered

---

HUCA 60 [1989] 15). The second exception is problematic. Its antecedent is *swsym*, horses, so the verb should have been *wyrmswh*, and they trampled her. If so, the *nun* may be an ancient scribal error for *waw*, a possibility in the ancient Hebrew script.

[7] Cf. the data collected by M. Held, "The YQTL-QTL (QTL-YQTL) Sequence of Identical Verbs in Biblical Hebrew and in Ugaritic," *Studies and Essays in Honor of Abraham A. Neuman* (eds. M. Ben-Horin et al.; Leiden: E. J. Brill, 1962) 281–90.

[8] I do not include six examples of *yqtl* past tense from the Deir 'Alla inscriptions because the classification of their dialect is uncertain. Cf. J. Hackett, *The Balaam Text From Deir 'Alla* (Harvard Semitic Museum Monograph 31; Chico, CA.: Scholars Press, 1984) 104; W. R. Garr, *Dialect Geography of Syria-Palestine, 1000–586 B.C.E.* (Philadelphia: University of Pennsylvania Press, 1985) 223–24, 229–31.

Examples from Hebrew, Moabite, and Phoenician on the one hand, and Hamathian and Danite (most likely Damascene) Aramaic on the other, indicate that they are not anomalous, no matter where the dialect is ultimately classified on a Canaanite-Aramaic continuum.

[9] This chapter's objective is to provide a synchronic description of the verbal system in written texts during the Iron Age. I refer to diachronic factors only to clarify elements on the synchronic plane.

only masoretic texts.[10] This evaluation of masoretic data, however, has been challenged.

In a detailed study of data bearing on these forms, L. McFall concluded that the distribution of the accent in *qatal* forms correlates neither with the presence or absence of a preceding *waw* nor with the time reference of the verb and is not, therefore, phonemic. Rather, he suggested, the placement of the tone marking accent is determined syntactically according to the position of the word in its "sense unit."[11]

A new analysis and evaluation of the extensive data presented by McFall suggest an alternative, but less stark, conclusion closer to the traditional position of Hebraists.

Johnson indicates that 6,378 occurrences of *we* + *qtl* forms are attested in the Bible, but most of these are non-diagnostic since the accent is fixed on the penultimate syllable.[12] McFall counted 1761 *we* + *qtl* + *ti/ta* forms in Mandelkern's concordance. Seven of the forms lack a tone because they are in bound constructions with a following word; 1295 have an ultimate tone and 459 have a penultimate tone.

Of the 1295 verbs with ultimate tone, 1284 or 99.15% had a "non-past" meaning in accordance with the *a priori* argument; however, eleven verbs did not.[13]

Of the 459 verbs with penultimate tone, 319 were either III *aleph* or III *he* (< III *w/y*), verbs that do not take an ultimate tone for phonetic reasons—*w'pyt* in Lev 24:5 is the only exception—and are therefore not relevant for

---

[10] Cf. McFall, *The Enigma*, 11, 190 and Joüon-Muraoka, *A Grammar of Biblical Hebrew*, 63, §15c.

Levita operated with a notion of the so-called *waw*-conversive that may no longer be maintained. As indicated at the beginning of this chapter, abundant examples from Hebrew supported by those from Moabite and Aramaic prose demonstrate that the presence or absence of the *waw* was irrelevant to the time reference of the verb.

[11] McFall, *The Enigma*, 190–91, 210.

I use "tone" to refer to the graphic mark developed by masoretes to designate the "stress" or "accent" of a word or group of words in their reading tradition.

[12] Johnson, *Hebräisches Perfekt*, 24. Johnson presents an extensive statistical breakdown of the distribution of relevant data.

[13] McFall presents examples of verbs accented on the final syllable that refer to past time: Lev 26:41; Deut 17:4; 1 Kgs 19:18; Jer 6:17; 12:3; 20:9; Ezek 29:7 and Amos 4:7 (*The Enigma*, p. 194 *ad* (4)). Only Jer 12:3 and Amos 4:7 are good examples. The others refer to present-future time or may be interpreted as doing so in context.

this analysis. There remain 140 verbs within this category useful for the survey. Of these, 72 verbs constituting 51% of the 140 indicate past time in accord with the argument, but 68 (= 49% of the 140), do not.[14]

These figures may be interpreted in four different ways:

1) All relevant verbs of both categories, 1295 *weqatalti/ta* verbs with ultimate tone + 140 with penultimate tone (= 1435) may be lumped together. Of these, 1367 (= 95% of the total) are marked properly and the traditional argument is essentially correct.

2) The argument is correct only for verbs marked to indicate present-future time but not past time.

3) The argument is correct only for verbs marked to indicate past time, but incorrect for verbs marked to indicate present-future time.

4) The argument is incorrect and an alternative explanation clarifying all relevant verbs may be proposed.

McFall opted for the fourth interpretation of the data, proposing that accent was conditioned syntactically. When *qatal* verbs, with or without the *waw*, were initial in a sense unit (i.e., a constituent unit of textual information delineated by a disjunctive masoretic tone in the word preceding the unit and the one concluding it), the accent was on the final syllable; when such verbs were placed at the end of a sense unit, the accent was on the penultimate syllable.[15] Noting that all examples of *wqtl* with an accent on the final syllable are in reported speech while none are found in narrative, he proposed that the distribution was due to the fact that "Direct Speech Style" differs from "Narrative Prose Style" in most languages with regard to pitch, modulation, expression, speed, animation, etc. "The Masoretic accent system would appear to capture this difference in the two styles, slight though that difference might appear at times."[16] This specific observation, however, is not particularly

---

[14] McFall, *The Enigma*, 191–93.

[15] McFall, *The Enigma*, 193– 94, 196.

[16] McFall, *The Enigma*, 193. This observation has anecdotal value alone unless accompanied by statistics describing the distribution of the two styles in those books where the forms are found. On the basis of intensive thumbing through the text, I estimate that over 50% of the Tanakh consists of direct and indirect speech. The remaining sections, with a few exceptions in post-exilic Ezra-Nehemiah, are 3rd person narratives where such forms are not to be expected.

relevant, since verbs with a penultimate accent are also found in direct speech contexts (e.g., 1 Sam 23:2; 29:8; 1 Kgs 2:31; 2 Kgs 9:3; Ezek 3:26). More significantly, the masoretic notations were not intended to recreate or preserve ancient patterns of natural or dramatic speech or, for that matter, even to delimit recognizable grammatical units such as conditional clauses or prepositional phrases.

Two assumptions underlie McFall's general conclusions, one articulated clearly but not employed consistently, and one implicit in his descriptions. The first is that the tone on the final syllable of *w'pyt*, "and you will bake," in Lev 24:5 shows that the final syllable of such words could be accented. Accordingly, more tones would have been placed in that position, were accent phonemic. Its almost uniform absence from that position in III *he* and III *aleph* verbs with a present-future meaning is, therefore, an indication that accent was not phonemic.[17] On the basis of this assumption, he is able to cite as evidence against the phonemic argument relevant conjugated forms of 163 III *he* and 36 III *aleph* verbs marked with a penultimate accent, even though they refer to present-future time. However, McFall also states elsewhere— correctly, in my opinion—that the accented, final syllable in *w'pyt* is best explained as due to analogy with the immediately preceding *wlqht*, "and you will take," in the same verse.[18] This observation undermines completely the significance of the exceptional *w'pyt* and all inferences derived from it to III *he* and analogically formed III *aleph* verbs, as well as any concomitant arguments based on it.

His second assumption is that the rules of syllable regression do not explain adequately the exceptions in which verbs accented on the penultimate syllable had a present-future meaning. McFall demonstrates that in cases where a monosyllabic word following a relevant verb form had a major disjunctive, i.e., *silluq* or *athnach*, the tone on the verb was penultimate in twelve out of sixteen examples. He attempts to refine this further by distinguishing between the disjunctive and conjunctive tone on the immediately preceding verb,

---

In making his observation, however, McFall crosses into text linguistics/discourse analysis and his point is noteworthy. Israelite authors representing spoken language marked it as such by forms and structures appropriate for and conventional to that language register. Thus, the theoretical ambiguity of the *qatal* form as perceived graphically in extant texts, biblical and extra-biblical, must be considered a recurring element within quotidian speech where I cannot assume that it was a constant source of potential ambiguity.

[17] McFall, *The Enigma*, 193–94

[18] McFall, *The Engima*, 197.

noting that the four exceptions bore disjunctive tones. In phrases or clauses smaller than the half-verse (i.e., not closed by a *silluq* or *athnach)*, when a minor disjunctive occurred on the final word, the pattern was clear: preceding verbs with disjunctives were accented on the final syllable; those with conjunctives were accented on either the final or penultimate one.[19] This lack of definition led him to propose the syntactic hypothesis.

However, if it is assumed that accent was phonemic in these verbs, McFall's exceptions may be explained by applying the notion of "override warrants" to the system of tones that included both primary, hierarchically ordered "syntactical" markers, the disjunctives, as well as secondary musical notations, the conjunctives, that were completely dependent on the syntactic ones. The whole system intended to preserve a tradition of liturgical recitation characterized by economic phrasing that usually, but not always, defined sense units broken down to immediate constituents.[20] At times, there was tension between traditional pronunciation, conventional phonological changes owing to word juxtapositions in the verse structure, syntactic phrasing, phrase length, and even in the patterning of the tone notations themselves.[21] Something had to give.

One tradition, usually that of phrasing for liturgical performance, overrode the others, creating variations in them, departures from the statistically common patterns. Thus, the first grammatical sentence in the Tanakh, beginning at *br'šyt*, "at the beginning of," and ending at *'wr*, "light," consists of 27

---

[19] McFall, *The Enigma*, 195–97. I present his data in a manner emphasizing the deviations. His presentation, though not the numbers, differs (cf. p. 195 *ad* (1)).

[20] I. Yeivin, *Introduction to the Tiberian Masorah* (translated and edited by E. J. Revell; Maoretic Studies 5; Missoula: Scholars Press, 1980) 218–28; S. Kogut, *Correlations Between Biblical Accentuation and Traditional Jewish Exegesis. Linguistic and Contextual Studies* (Hebrew; Jerusalem: Magnes Press and The Hebrew University, 1994) 13–29.

M. B. Cohen has proposed that in Isa 40:5, 13; 45:1, the system may have been manipulated by masoretes, in the manner of scribal emendations, to avoid theologically inappropriate phrases ("Masoretic Accents as Biblical Commentary," *JANESCU* 4 [1972] 3–11). His examples are interesting but too few to undermine general statements about the system as a whole. S. Kogut, however, provides many examples of Jewish exegesis from late antiquity through the high Middle Ages that interpreted passages in a manner at variance with the meaning implicit in the parsing of the tones (*Correlations*, 111–250).

[21] For this latter point, cf. Yeivin, *Introduction*, 169–72. The tones were sometimes influenced by musical considerations, a phenomenon inferred from the data but incapable of demonstration since the musical system employed is not known (cf. pp. 159, 233–35).

words. The sentence is divided into three liturgical verses, Gen 1:1–3 consisting of seven, fourteen, and six words respectively. Conversely, one of the two accentuation systems for the ten commandments creates a single verse from syntactically distinct units in Exod 20:2–5, 8–11, while the other bundles Exod 20:13–16 into a single liturgical unit.[22] Psalms 1:1–3; 5:11–13; 125:2–3 all comprise single sentences broken down into smaller liturgical units; Psalms 2:4, 7; 3:2, 6; 4:2, 5 all contain two or more grammatical sentences combined in a single verse.[23]

Another override phenomenon is discernible in the retraction of an ultimate accent to the penultimate syllable when followed directly by an accented syllable. This regression for euphonic reasons, termed *nāsōg 'āḥōr* in masoretic parlance, could result in the resyllabification of words and the lengthening of vowels. Such accent retraction is attested between two words, e.g., Gen 1:5; 3:19; 19:27; 45:1; but not in Exod 29:5; 40:3; Deut 21:11; 23:14.[24] In long words, *nāsōg 'āḥōr* sometimes resulted in the development of secondary accents, e.g., Num 28:26; Isa 55:9. It operated in phrases as well, e.g., Gen 3:19; Ezek 33:12.[25]

---

[22] M. B. Cohen and D. B. Freedman, "The Dual Accentuation of the Ten Commandments," *Masoretic Studies* 1 (1974) 7–19, provide a competent interpretation for the origin of this phenomena building on the observation of Ibn Habib, who distinguished between a private reading that broke the commandments into smaller units and a public one that bunched syntactic units together.

Aside from the ten commandments, dual accentuation is attested only in Gen 35:22. One accentual pattern considers the whole a single verse; the other marks one verse ending after the word Israel and a second at the end of v. 22. Here, however, it has been explained as due to different interpretations of the text. Cf. T. Hazoniel, "The Doubled Accents of Genesis 35:22," *Beit Mikra* 42 (1996) 66–67, 80 (Hebrew).

[23] Z. Zevit, "Cognitive Theory and the Memorability of Biblical Poetry," *Maarav* 8 (1992) 205–08.

[24] Most of these negative examples involve diagnostic *qataltá* forms. In Deut 21:11a, 23:14b they have disjunctive accents.

[25] Blau, *A Grammar*, 18; G. Bergsträsser, *Hebräische Grammatik I* (Hildesheim: Georg Olms, 1962; originally published Leipzig, 1918]) 69–73, §11; 127–28, §21cc. (Bergsträsser also notes that masoretic manuscripts representing the Ben Naftali tradition regularly indicate secondary stress in closed syllables, unlike the Ben Asher tradition.) Yeivin, *Introduction*, 236–40; Z. Zevit, "Nondistinctive Stress, Syllabic Constraints, and Wortmetrik in Ugaritic Poetry," *UF* 15 (1983) 295–98; E. J. Revell, "The Conditioning of Stress Position in *Waw* Consecutive Perfect Forms in Biblical Hebrew," *HAR* 9 (1985) 277–300; Waltke and O'Connor, *Biblical Hebrew Syntax*, 520–21.

The euphonic override of phonemic accents clarifies the displacement attested in the following verses with diagnostic *qaltí/qatalá* forms: Exod 25:12; Lev 26:25, 35; Deut 14:26; 26:1; 28:36, 64, 68; 2 Sam 9:10; 1 Kgs 22:13; Jer 17:27; 21:14; 24:10; 43:12; 49:26; Ezek 14:13; 17:22; 28:12, 22, 25; 30:14, 16; 32:8; 35:11; 39:27. This displacement is attested even with minor disjunctives within the verse, e.g., Deut 32:40; 1 Sam 20:18; Jer 4:1–2, but these comprise an exceptional category rather than the rule.[26]

Despite inconsistencies, such as those described in the preceding paragraphs, masoretic tones contribute significantly toward comprehending the role of phonemic accent. Accordingly, I accept the first interpretation of McFall's raw data, namely, that accent placement on *weqatalti/ta* verbs was intended to mark the time reference of the verbs.[27] This interpretation has the added advantage of accommodating relevant data from cognate languages.

Extra-biblical data support the phonemic argument. *Qatal* 2 m.s. verbal forms referring to future time are attested in the Arad inscriptions: *whsbt*, "and you will 'inspect'" (*AI* 2:5–6); *wntt*, "and you will give" (*AI* 2:8); *wṣrrt*, "and you will bind" (*AI* 3:5); and *wlqḥt*, "and you will take" (*AI* 17:3–4). They are all written defectively and contrast orthographically with forms referring to past time: *ktbth*, "you wrote" (*AI* 7:6); and *yd'th*, "you knew" (*AI* 40:9). The form *yd'th* in a Lachish letter (*KAI* 192:6) may also be interpreted this way, though most students of the letters interpret the final *he*

Shakespeare's departures from the iambic pentameter may be explained as arising from similar override warrants. Depending on the deviation and the dramatic moment, performers sometimes remold the words to fit the meter by skipping or slurring a syllable; or they pause, deliver the line in a slower cadence, and then resume the Elizabethan diction.

26 The examples in this and the preceding paragraph are taken from I. Ben-David, *Contextual and Pausal Forms in Biblical Hebrew. Syntax and Accentuation* (Hebrew; Jerusalem: Magnes Press, 1995) 277. Ben-David develops an explanatory hypothesis for deviating forms with disjunctive accents on the basis of syntactic and phonological-phonetic constraints and warrants. (Cf. pp. 5–8, 27, and pp. x–xii in the English summary.)

27 E. J. Revell similarly critiques McFall's innovative work for relying on the tone system as a key to semantic and syntactic structure and for assuming that the accent of *qatalti/ta* forms was conditioned by the style of the context ("The Conditioning of Stress Position," 278). He does allow, however, that syntax and semantics strongly influenced the liturgical reading tradition because they determined naturally the phonetic patterning and the parsing clusters of clauses and phrases (p. 280). I concur that this is often, if not usually, the case. Nevertheless, as indicated above, the liturgical patterning which created clusters of three-four lexical units did not necessarily coincide with natural or logical divisions.

as an objective pronoun: "you did not know it."[28] The orthographic distinction in these documents coincides with and, perhaps, was intended to mark the difference in accent between past and present-future forms.[29]

The main arguments for the originally phonemic status of stress in distinguishing between the time references of the *qatal* verbs therefore are the following: 1) the general correspondence of marked accents with the different time references in diagnostic forms; 2) attestation of such phonemic stress in verbs of the *yiqtol* pattern; and 3) the necessity of positing some distinguishing feature in classical Hebrew, imagined as a living language, that would not have appeared as a matter of course in the orthography of the language as it developed historically.

Ostensibly, the syntax of most of these verbs in biblical narrative—not in the masoretic groupings of immediate constituents—contests the phonemic argument. The verbs often occur in sentences after a verb, or a quasi-verbal set-up, indicating present-future time and referring to an action attendant on circumstances posited by the first verb or the set-up but consecutive to it. Here they have a telic or consequential role indicating "and then / and so / and therefore." Cf. the following examples:

Gen 3:5
> ...on the day of your eating from it, *wnpqḥw 'ynykm*, and then your eyes will be opened (or, will open themselves—zz).

Gen 6:14
> ...make the ark with chambers, *wkprt 'th*, and then you will cover it with pitch....

Gen 7:4
> ...I am causing rain on the earth..., *wmḥyty*, and so I will blot out....

Gen 24:4
> Indeed, to my land and my birthplace you will go, *wlqḥt*, and then you will take a wife for my son.

---

[28] E.g., W. Nebe, "Zu Lachisch Ostracon 2," *ZAH* 9 (1996) 48. The common interpretation reflects, of course, the existing consensus about the system.

[29] Z. Zevit, *Matres Lectionis in Ancient Hebrew Epigraphs* (ASOR Monograph Series 2; USA: ASOR, 1980) 31–32.

In biblical Hebrew, the picture is more complicated and overlayed than my remarks in *Matres Lectionis* indicate. Compare the data presented in J. Barr, *The Variable Spellings of the Hebrew Bible* (New York: Oxford University Press, 1989) 114–27.

Exod 6:6–7
I am YHWH, *whwṣ'ty 'tkm...whṣlty...wg'lty...wlqḥty 'tkm ly l'm*, and
therefore I will take you out...and will rescue...and will redeem...and will take
you for myself for a people....

Exod 21:12–13
He who smites a man, and the man dies will be put to death; and (concerning—
zz) one who did not stalk but God caused it to happen, *wśmty*, and then I will
establish a place for you to which he may flee.

Lev 4:3
If the anointed priest sin..., *whqryb*, and then he will offer in addition to his
purification offering....

1 Sam 10:2
In (the circumstance of—zz) your going from me today, *wmṣ't*, and then you
will find two men..., *w'mrw*, and then they will say to you....

Jer 12:3
And you YHWH knew me; you see me, *wbḥnt*, and then you test my heart.[30]

These data, however, comprise an insufficient argument against the
phonemic explanation. *Qatal* past tense verbs occur in the same syntactical
position with a telic or consequential sense, a fact that seriously compromises
the argument from syntax. Cf. the following:

Judg 3:23
...and Ehud went out to the corridor, and he closed the doors of the upper
chamber behind himself, *wn'l*, and then he locked (them—zz).

Judg 16:18
...She called to the Philistine princes saying "Ascend now because he told me
all," *w'lw*, and then they ascended....

---

[30] Waltke and O'Connor catalogue the syntactic placement of *qatal* present-future verbs in
prose (*Biblical Hebrew Syntax*, 525–38). If, perhaps, somewhat overly refined, their catalogue indicates beyond doubt that *qatal* present-future verbs were not in free variation with
yiqtól verbs, a situation that might have given rise to ambiguity and confusion.

R. E. Longacre suggests that they were conditioned by the discourse conventions of
ancient Israel. According to him, the most common use of *weqatal* forms was in predictive,
procedural, and instructional discourse ("Weqatal Forms in Biblical Hebrew Prose: A
Discourse-modular Approach," *Biblical Hebrew and Discourse Linguistics* [ed. R. D.
Bergen; USA: Summer Institute of Linguistics, 1994] 50–54). Longacre does not distinguish
between forms with a past and those with a present-future meaning.

1 Kgs 20:21
...and he smote the cavalry and the chariotry, *whkh*, and so he smote Aram greatly.

2 Kgs 14:7
He smote Edom in the Valley of Salt, ten thousand (men—*zz*), *wtpś*, and then captured Sela in the battle.

The phonemic argument, therefore, serves also to explain how *weqatal* verbs in the same syntactic context were distinguished from each other as well as how present-future *qatal* verbs were distinguished originally when not preceded by a *waw*, e.g., *ntty* (Gen 15:18; 23:11; 48:22), *ydʿty* (Gen 27:2), *hgdty* (Deut 26:3), *lqḥty* (1 Sam 2:16), *ʿśyty* (2 Sam 14:11), *yʿṣty* (2 Sam 17:11), *śnʾty* (Jer 44:4), *ʿmdty* (1 Kgs 17:1; Job 30:20), *ndmyty* (Isa 6:5), *qnyty* (Ruth 4:9).[31] Note also the non-diagnostic *lmʿn yrʾtm* (Josh 4:24) "so that you will fear YHWH your God forever."

Nothing in the syntax of the various contexts in which these occur precludes the use of a *yiqtól* form, so it cannot be maintained as a strong argument that they were conditioned syntactically or that their tense is a function of syntax.[32] Although the number of examples is small and the conditions under which these verbs were used has not yet been described, it appears that they were restricted neither by literary genre nor by syntactic structure in Hebrew. Therefore, the phonemic explanation is easily extended to clarify examples of the so-called prophetic or precative perfect, usually explained by recourse to aspect.[33]

---

[31] Fenton, "Hebrew 'Tenses'," 35–36 considers these forms in diachronic perspective. In the extant text, they are generally not accented on the final syllable.

[32] Y. Endo concludes on the basis of a limited corpus, the Joseph story complex, that the position of a verb in clause initial or non-clause initial position affects neither temporal nor aspectual matters (*The Verbal System of Classical Hebrew in the Joseph Story. An Approach from Discourse Analysis* [The Netherlands: Van Gorcum, 1996] 320).

[33] The very existence of the prophetic perfect as a real grammatical category is debated; among those who consider it to be real, there is much disagreement about parade examples (I. W. Provan, "Past, present and future in Lamentations iii 52–66: the case for a precative perfect reexamined," *VT* 41 [1991] 164–67). G. L. Klein has studied 43 passages to which the category has been applied. He contends that of these only fifteen contain *qtl* verbs indicating future time. Only these, incapable of alternative explanations according to his criteria, are assigned properly to this category: Gen 17:20; Num 24:17; Isa 5:13; 9:1–5; 10:28; 11:9; 19:7; 43:14; 48:41; Jer 51:30 (?); Dan 7:27 ("The Prophetic Perfect," *JNSL* 16 [1990] 48–59). Similarly, Provan rests his case for the usefulness of the category "precative perfect" on the interpretation of Lam 3:52–56, concluding that it is useful ("Past, present, and future," 175). Though far

Similar examples are attested in Phoenician-Punic both with and without a preceding *waw*. The earliest is from the eighth century BCE Karatepe inscription:

KAI 26 A III:12–IV:1
> If a king...or any man effaces the name of Azitawadda from this gate..., *wmḥ b'lšmm w'l qn 'rṣ*, and then will they (i.e., the following list of gods—zz) Baal Shamem and El Creator of Earth efface that man.

CIS i 3783.5–6
> *wkl 'dm 'š gnb t-mtnt z nkst tnt [p]n b'l*, as for any person who will steal this gift, Thinnith-Phanebal shall kill him.

CIS i 4945.4–6
> *w 'š yrgz t-mtnt z wqbt tnt pn b'l*, as for anybody who disturbs this gift, Thinnith-Phanebal shall curse him.

CIS i 165.20
> *kl khn 'š yqḥ mš't bdṣ l'š št bps z wn'nš*, as for any priest who receives payment contrary to what is specified in this inscription, he shall be fined.[34]

These examples demonstrate that the *qatal* present-future tense is not unique to Hebrew in the Northwest Semitic language group.[35] Extending this observation justifies hypothesizing that what is claimed for the *yiqtol* part of the proto-Hebrew-Phoencian verbal system with regard to tense is equally valid for the *qatal* part.

The preceding conclusion accounts adequately for tense in the verbal system of biblical Hebrew, but not aspect; it does not constitute a complete description of the verbal system. The following brief remarks are intended,

---

from exhaustive, these studies are serviceable beginnings for clarifying this problematic category.

[34] The Phoenician-Punic examples are cited from C. Krahmalkov, "The *Qatal* with Future Tense Reference in Phoenician," *JSS* 31 (1986) 5–10. Cf. also Segert, *A Grammar*, 193, §64.422. For a discussion of the verbal forms *nkst*, "she will kill him," and *qbt*, "she shall curse him," cf. P. C. Schmitz, "A Problem of Punic Morphology: The Third Person Singular Feminine of the Suffixing Conjugation with Affixed Object Pronoun," *JSS* 40 (1995) 219–25.

M. Smith lists examples of *qtl* as a performative perfective that indicates present time and a precative perfect representing future time in Ugaritic ("The **qatala* Form in Ugaritic Narrative Poetry," 795–99) while W. L. Moran cites examples from Amarna Akkadian that may reflect the Canaanite substrata ("The Hebrew Language in Its Northwest Semitic Background," *The Bible and the Ancient Near East: Essays in Honor of William Foxwell Albright* (ed. G. E. Wright; Garden City: Doubleday, 1961) 64–65).

[35] As a consequence, the history of this form with its distinguishing accent phoneme cannot be reconstructed for Hebrew alone and remains to be worked out.

therefore, to remedy this by sketching how the description may be rounded out.

Aspect in Hebrew is expressed/indicated morphosemantically through various forms:

a) Stativity is partially marked in the *Qal* stem by the *qātōl* and *qātēl* patterns.

b) Factitive, resultative, frequentive, reflexive, causative, etc. meanings are expressed through the *Niphal, Piel, Hiphil*, and *Hithpael* stems.

c) Passivity (+/- the meanings adduced in b) is marked by the *Pual, Hophal*, and sometimes by the *Niphal* stems. These are all grammaticized.

d) Continuity is expressed by *hālōk* + absolute infinitive (cf. Gen 6:1; 10:18; Judg 20:39; 1 Sam 14:35) and may be considered lex-icalized, but also through subordinate participial clauses, i.e., through syntax.

Other features are inherent in the *Aktionsart* of individual verbs and are "activated" through the interplay between lexical semantics, particularly in the *Qal*, the undifferentiated, base stem, and pragmatic contexts.[36] Aspect is thus independent of the tense system.

Similarly, mood, an expression of the subjective attitude of the speaker, is sometimes grammaticized through the use of imperative, jussive, and cohorta-tive verbal forms. Urgency and emphasis may be expressed through lexical-ization by the particle *nā'* after imperatives, by the infinitive absolute of a conjugated verb form used before or after the verb, and by the use of the *nun-energicum* with certain forms of the *yiqtol present-future*. It may also be ex-

---

[36] These remarks are cursory and are intended to be incompletely suggestive rather than completely descriptive. I suspect that a study of Hebrew aspect will be even more frustrating than that of tense. C. Bache's intensive study of English aspect and tense, an attempt to produce a well defined technical vocabulary by which phenomena in all languages relevant to these categories may be described, results in complex compatabililty and constraint rules. It is suggestive of what may be necessary for Hebrew (*The Study of Aspect, Tense and Action. Towards a Theory of the Semantics of Grammatical Categories* [Frankfurt am Main: Peter Lang, 1995] 317–35).

pressed through syntax, as in the case of conditional clauses.[37] Most often, however, mood is not expressed explicitly in an unambiguous, formal way and must be understood as situationally determined. Mood may therefore be discerned—and there is a strong subjective element to this procedure— through a consideration of the semantics and pragmatics of each literary context.[38] Thus, in Hebrew, it appears that some of the congeries of devices for expressing mood piggyback on part of the tense system.

* * *

When some Hebrew dialects first tended to shift word stress toward their first syllable in the post-exilic period, the *qatal* present-future became potentially ambiguous. Except for certain frozen expressions such as *ntty, qnyty, lqhty*, commercial terms, and in certain syntactic constructions, people preferred not to use the *qatal* present-future tense. It is poorly attested in late Hebrew texts.[39] The decline in usage was possible because the *qatal* present-future was redundant within the verbal system as a whole and because of changing linguistic usage. Its decline, reflecting changing linguistic habits, did not affect the communicative efficacy of the verbal system at all. By 100 BCE, *qtl* functioned mainly as a past tense. Hebrew had become less tensed, but not untensed.

The preceding description of the Hebrew verbal system during the Iron Age may prove to be more useful than others in tracing the evolution of the system into that of Mishnaic Hebrew, ca. 200 CE. The most obvious difference is the disappearance of *we + qtl* present-future and *wa + yqtl* past verbs in narrative sequences. In Mishnaic Hebrew, past time was indicated by *qatal*;

---

[37] Some of these topics, e.g., particles and the infinitive absolute, are dealt with extensively in the important work of T. Muraoka, *Emphatic Words and Structures in Biblical Hebrew* (Leiden: Brill and Jerusalem: Magnes Press, 1985) 83–92, 113–64. Muraoka notes that many emphatic forms are found in emotionally charged contexts in reported speech (pp. 165–66). These, in particular, are relevant to a discussion of mood.

[38] Cf. E. J. Revell's description and analysis of modal forms in "The System of the Verb," 13–32. His study negotiates well between the Hebrew forms and English (mis)representation so that it has contrastive value. Much of what is explained in traditional grammars by recourse to "aspect" is clarified by Revell as due to the misunderstood use of tenses or through a consideration of modal valences read out of pragmatic situations presupposed in the text (pp. 2, 32–33). His conclusions about mood will have to be factored into any comprehensive tense-based description of classical Hebrew.

[39] McFall, *The Enigma*, appendix 1, table 2 (no pagination).

present-future time by *qōtel*, a verbalized participle qualified formally by pronouns and adverbs, and informally by pragmatics; absolute future was indicated by *'ātīd* + *l* + infinitive. *Yqtl* was used to express various moods such as obligation, willingness, and subjunctivity. Repetitive, durative, and continuous actions in the past were indicated by *hyh* + *qōtel*, in the future by *yhyh* + *qōtel*; punctual events were indicated in the past by *qōtel* + *hyh*, in the future by *qōtel yhyh*.

In the evolved verbal system, linear time was indicated by both grammaticized and lexicalized forms. *Qtl* emerged as the main line narrative tense. This may have developed out of informal speech patterns at the end of the Iron Age since it is already attested as a narrative tense in some 7th–6th centuries BCE Hebrew texts: 2 Kgs 23:4, 5, 8, 10, 12, 14, 15; Jer 7:31; 18:4; 19:4, 5; etc. The polyvalent *yqtl* of biblical Hebrew became restricted in function as other structures took over (or, overtook) its tense function.[40]

The "new" compound forms mixed grammatical, lexical, and syntactic conventions to mark aspect as the resources of the earlier periods were reorganized into a less ambiguous and redundant system during the Persian and Hellenistic periods. Factors contributing to or influencing these changes may have been 1) phonetic changes, 2) a tendency to shift stress to the head of words, 3) a preference for S + V syntactic ordering, 4) the growing prestige of Galileean Hebrew dialects with their own complex histories,[41] 4) the influence of Aramaic and, perhaps, 5) the influence of Greek.

---

[40] Kutscher, *A History*, 125–32; M. Mishor, *The Tense System in Tannaitic Hebrew* (Hebrew; Ph.D. thesis submitted to the Hebrew University of Jerusalem, 1983) 155–84; 351–400; Azar, *The Syntax of Mishnaic Hebrew*, 1–19 and notes 2, 3, 7, 8.

[41] A sense of this complexity is conveyed in G. A. Rendsberg, "The Galilean Background of Mishnaic Hebrew," *The Galilee in Late Antiquity* (ed., L. I. Levine; New York and Jerusalem: The Jewish Theological Seminary of America, 1992) 225–37.

VII

THE EMERGENCE OF THE ANTERIOR CONSTRUCTION

Recognizing that Hebrew verbs indicate tense, it is possible to suggest broadly how the anterior construction may have emerged.

The verbal system of Semitic languages considered as a family is less complicated than that of the Slavic family and hence less able to make the subtle distinctions noted in Russian and even the simpler ones marked in English. Furthermore, the Hebrew system, along with that of other West Semitic languages, is even less complicated than that which evolved in East Semitic. So, when Israelite authors sought to indicate the past to the past retrospectively within narrative traditionally composed through linked syndetic constructions, they faced a daunting problem.

In certain contexts they could indicate pluperfect through a subordinate *k'šr* clause employing a *qatal* past tense verb in which the chronological displacement was obvious:

Gen 7:9
> Two by two they came to Noah to the ark, male and female, *k'šr ṣwh 'lyhm 't nḥ*, as God commanded (i.e., had commanded) Noah (cf. Gen 7:5).

Exod 1:17
> And the midwives feared God and did not do, *k'šr dbr 'lyhn mlk mṣrym*, as the king of Egypt instructed (i.e., had instructed) them....

Judg 1:20
> and they gave Hebron to Caleb, *k'šr dbr mšh*, as Moses said (i.e., had said before they gave it)....

1 Kgs 11:38
> If you listen to all that I command you and walk in my ways and do that which is right in my eyes..., *k'šr 'šh dwd 'bdy*, as did David my servant....

The overwhelming majority of such examples occur with the verbs of speech *'mr, ṣwh, dbr*, e.g., Gen 7:16, 21; 12:4; 17:23; 21:1; 27:19; Exod 7:6, 10, 13,

20, 22; 13:11; 17:10; 39:1, 57 etc. The past to the past meaning is attested with other verbs but rarely, e.g., *'śh* (Gen 8:21), *hqryb* (Gen 12:11), *ṭm'* (Gen 34:13), *śrp* (Lev 4:21), *q'h* (Lev 18:28), *n'sp* (Num 27:13), *zmm* (Deut 19:19), *ntn* (Jos 1:15), *hpk* (2 Kgs 5:26). However, *k'šr* + *qatal* past does not indicate this meaning in Gen 24:22; 27:4, 14, 30; 29:10; 30:25; 32:32; 37:23; Exod 32:19; Deut 6:16; 28:63; Judg 7:5; 1 Sam 12:8; 15:33; 2 Sam 16:19; 1 Kgs 3:6; 20:34. The semantic of the construction is therefore not lexicalized but varies according to context.

As a rough rule of thumb, when *k'šr* may be translated "as/like" in a context involving comparisons, the *qatal* verb may sometime refer to a pluperfect situation; but when renderable as "when" in temporal clauses, it is a simple past. However, even in contexts where a pluperfect sense is obvious, primarily in the case of speech verbs, the verb alludes to a prior event in the narrative and does not present the prior event itself. Therefore, these clauses are significantly different from the retrospective ones within the narrative that comprise the focus of this research. *K'šr* clauses were neither developed nor adapted to fill this role.

In some contexts, Israelite authors indicated that one event had occurred prior to an event just described by employing clauses using *ky*, "because," + verb:

Gen 32:21
> And you will also say (to Esau), "and lo, our servant Jacob is behind us," *ky 'mr*, because he thought, "I will appease him...."

Gen 38:11
> And Judah said to Tamar his daughter-in-law, "Dwell...in your father's house until Shelah my son grows up," *ky 'mr*, because he thought, "Lest he die like his brothers"....

Judg 16:18
> And Delilah saw that he told her all that was in his heart, so she sent and called to the lords of the Philistines saying, "Come up now," *ky hgyd lh* (reading with the *ketib*—zz), because he told her all that was in his heart....

1 Sam 14:1–3
> ...and Jonathan said to the young man, bearer of his arms, "Let us go and cross over to the Philistine fortification..." and he did not tell his father—and Saul was staying at the edge of the hill...in Migron, and the people with him, about six hundred men, and Ahijah...was priest in Shiloh...—and the people did not know, *ky hlk*, that Jonathan went.

1 Kgs 3:10

And the matter was good in the eyes of the Lord, *ky š'l*, that Solomon requested that thing (i.e., wisdom).

Jonah 1:10

And the people feared a great fear and they said to him, "What is this that you have done!" because the people knew that from before YHWH he fled, *ky hgyd lhm*, because he told them.

Job 1:5

...and he rose early in the morning and made offerings..., *ky 'mr*, because Job thought, "perhaps my children sinned...."

These examples are all circumstantial clauses in which the pluperfect sense is occasioned by virtue of the placement of the clause after the particular behavior that it is meant to clarify: Gen 16:13; 19:32; 21:16; 42:4; Exod 2:22; 13:17; 18:3; Deut 9:25; 1 Sam 1:22; 13:19; 20:26; 2 Sam 18:18; Hos 2:7; Esth 8:1. In most of these examples, the *ky* + *verb* clauses could have been placed intact at the head of their sentences. It is most likely coincidental that the verb *'mr* refers to thought rather than speech in most examples of this type where it occurs.

Neither the option of *k'šr* or *ky* clauses suited most contexts. A third option used by the ancient authors was to present the events out of order, assuming that the reader/listener would be able to discern the proper order— cf. the example cited above: (1a) John fell. (1b) Max pushed him. This would have been expressed in Hebrew as "and he-fell John and he-pushed him Max." Biblical Hebrew provides a number of examples of such scrambled sequencing:

Exod 4:31

(a) *wy'mn h'm* (b) *wyšm'w*
(a) and believed the people (b) and they heard that YHWH (had paid attention to the children of Israel....)

Exod 16:20

(a) *wyrm twl'ym* (b) *wyb'š*,
(a) and it bred maggots (b) and it stank

Lev 1:15

(a) *whqtyr hmzbḥh* (b) *wnmṣh dmw*,
(a) and he will turn it to smoke on the altar (b) and (it) shall be drained out its blood

Lev 9:22
(a) *wyś' 'hrn 't ydyw 'l h'm wybrkm* (b) *wyrd m'śt hḥṭ't wh'wlh whślmym,*
(a) and he lifted Aaron his hands to the people and he blessed them (b) and he descended from doing the purification, the burnt, and the well-being offerings

Isa 64:4
(a) *hn 'th qṣpt* (b) *wnḥṭ',*
(a) lo, you were angry (b) and we sinned

In all of these examples, (b) logically precedes (a) and indeed is prerequisite for it. Similarly, Exod 4:19 logically precedes 4:18; Exod 4:20b precedes 4:20a; Exod 18:6 precedes 18:5; Num 1:48–57 precedes 1:47; 1 Sam 17:21 precedes 17:20; 1 Kgs 13:12b precedes 12a; Isa 39:1b precedes 1a (cf. 1 Kgs 20:12).

These examples of scrambled sequencing, along with the *ky + verb* ones presented above, exhibit chronological slippage and are akin to afterthought, where an omitted detail is tacked on outside of the logical syntactic sequence:

Gen 14:12a
(a) and they took Lot and his possessions, (b) the son of Abram's brother (c) and they departed.

Num 13:23
(a) And they came to Wadi Eshqol and they cut from there a branch and a cluster of grapes (b) and they carried it by means of a beam (held) by two (c) and from the pomegranates and from the figs.

Judg 3:9
(a) ...and YHWH raised up a deliverer for the children of Israel (b) and he delivered them (c) Othniel son of Qenaz

1 Sam 18:4
(a) and Jonathan stripped off the cloak that was on him (b) and gave it to David (c) and his tunic and even his sword and even his bow and even his belt.

1 Kgs 2:32

(a) ...he who struck down two men better and more righteous than he (b) and he killed them by a sword and my father David had not known (c) Abner son of Ner...and Amasa son of Yeter....

In these examples, the informative content of the verse could have been more coherent had the (c) clause been placed after the (a) clause.[1]

The difference between these examples of afterthought and the preceding ones is that whereas these are awkward, slowing down the parsing process that extracts meaning from an utterance, they remain unambiguous. Information in the (c) clause loops back to the (a) clause naturally, either because it continues a sequence of activities, e.g., Gen 14:12; Num 13:23; 1 Sam 18:4, or because a noun/pronoun appositional link coheres the two, e.g., Judg 3:9; 1 Kgs 2:32.

Narratives indicating the past to the past by dischronologizing whole sentences or clauses within sentences were disconcerting and bordered on the unintelligible. Although the disconcerting quality may have attracted attention to the phenomenon, causing members of an audience to focus attentively on what was being portrayed, the quality of unintelligibility rendered it of dubious literary or rhetorical value. Passages in which simple dischronologization occurred could have been perceived as poorly formed or substandard or erroneous. Some may have been missed entirely since they are unremarkable syntactically. Furthermore, they lack stylistic panache.

Israelite writers developed an optional strategy to mark such cases specifically and unambiguously in narratives about the past. They created sentences of the type "and he-fell John and Max he-pushed him," (= John fell; Max had pushed him). In these sentences, the change in constituent ordering from *verb + subject* to *subject + verb* along with the introduction of a new subject became a conventional signal marking the retrospective anteriority of the clause.[2] It enabled them to translate more easily what they knew, what existed

---

[1] Gottstein presented examples of what he labeled the "afterthought-relative construction" in which relative clauses were detached from their head noun, e.g., Gen 22:14; 34:13; Deut 4:19; Judg 21:19; 2 Sam 7:12; 1 Kgs 3:19; 8:33; 10:10; Isa 29:22 ("Afterthought and the Syntax of Relative Clauses," 38–47).

[2] Cf. Muraoka, in Joüon-Muraoka, *A Grammar of Biblical Hebrew*, 390–91. Although the resultant clause was coordinated formally with the preceding information, it cannot be

inchoately in consciousness, into a linear narrative. In doing so, writers evolved a device that thickened the texture of their tales by manipulating the chronological flow of events, by indicating parallel and intersecting chains of events, and by hinting at the existence of untold narratives.[3]

The description of the preceding paragraph is generic rather than historical. Moabite and Phoenician examples adduced in chapter III indicate a more complex history for this construction, but extant data do not suffice to support serious speculation about it.

---

described properly as either coordinate—it has a different subject—or subordinate—it has its own subject and predicate—on the syntactic level, as described briefly above in chapter I.

Z. Livnat and M. Sela argue that in addition to coordination and subordination, a third relation may be posited for the relationship between elements in an utterance, namely, that of clarification. Although applying this notion to appositional information exclusively, their study creates new possibilities for exploring and describing the semantic-syntactic relationship between adjoined or juxtaposed clauses, including those employing the anterior construction ("Apposition–The Third Relation?" *Leš* 59 [1995] 60–68 [Hebrew]).

[3] This construction became only one of the means by which Israelite authors manipulated time in their narratives. Cf. S. Talmon, "The Presentation of Synchroneity and Simultaneity in Biblical Narrative," ScrHier 27 (1978) 9–26; Sternberg, *Poetics of Biblical Narrative*, 264–70; S. Bar-Efrat, *Narrative Art in the Bible* (JSOTSup 70; Sheffield: Almond Press, 1989) 143–84.

BIBLIOGRAPHY

Alter, R.
Genesis. New York: W. W. Norton & Co., 1996.

Andersen, F. I.
The Sentence in Biblical Hebrew. The Hague: Mouton, 1974.

Auerbach, E.
Mimesis: The Representation of Reality in Western Literature. Princeton, NJ: Princeton University Press, 1953.

Azar, M.
The Syntax of Mishnaic Hebrew (Hebrew). Jerusalem: The Academy of the Hebrew Language; University of Haifa, 1995.

Bache, C.
The Study of Aspect, Tense and Action. Towards a Theory of the Semantics of Grammatical Categories. Frankfurt am Main: Peter Lang, 1995.

Bar-Efrat, S.
Narrative Art in the Bible. JSOTSup 70. Sheffield: Almond, 1989.

Barr, J.
The Variable Spellings of the Hebrew Bible. New York: Oxford University Press, 1989.

Ben-David, I.
Contextual and Pausal Forms in Biblical Hebrew. Syntax and Accentuation (Hebrew). Jerusalem: Magnes Press, 1995.

Ben-Hayyim, Z.
"Samaritan Hebrew–An Evaluation." In *The Samaritans*, edited by A. D. Crown, 517–30. Tübingen: J. C. B. Mohr (Paul Siebeck), 1989.

Bergen, R. D.
Biblical Hebrew and Discourse Linguistics. USA: Summer Institute of Linguistics, 1994.

Bergsträsser, G.
Hebräische Grammatik I. Hildesheim: Georg Olms, Verlagsbuchhandlung, 1962. (First published, Leipzig, 1918.)

Hebräische Grammatik II, Teil: Verbum. Leipzig: J. C. Hinrichs Buchhandlung, 1929.

Berlin, A.
Poetics and Interpretation of Biblical Narrative. Sheffield: Almond Press, 1983.

Binnick, R. I.
Time and the Verb. A Guide to Tense and Aspect. New York: Oxford University Press, 1991.

Biran, A. and Naveh, J.
"The Tel Dan Inscription: A New Fragment," *IEJ* 45 (1995) 1–18.

Blau, J.
A Grammar of Biblical Hebrew. Wiesbaden: O. Harrasowitz, 1976.

"Marginalia Semitica III," *IOS* 7 (1977) 14–32.

"Pronominal Third Person Singular Suffixes With and Without N in Biblical Hebrew" ErIsr 14 (1978) 125–31 (Hebrew).

Buth, R.
"Methodological Collision Between Source Criticism and Discourse Analysis: The Problem of 'Unmarked Temporal Overlay' and the Pluperfect/Nonsequential *wayyiqtol.*" In *Biblical Hebrew and Discourse Linguistics,* edited by R. D. Bergen, 138–54. USA: Summer Institute of Linguistics, 1994.

Bybee, J. L.
Morphology. A Study of the Relationship Between Meaning and Form. Amsterdam: John Benjamin's Publishing, 1985.

Bybee, J., Perkins, R., and Pagliuca, W.
The Evolution of Grammar. Tense, Aspect and Modality in the Languages of the World. Chicago: University of Chicago Press, 1994.

Clifford, J. E.
Tense and Tense Logic. The Hague: Mouton, 1975.

Cohen, M. B.
"Masoretic Accents as Biblical Commentary," *JANESCU* 4 (1972) 2–11.

Cohen, M. B. and Freedman, D. B.
"The Dual Accentuation of the Ten Commandments," *Masoretic Studies* 1 (1974) 7–19.

Comrie, B.
Aspect. An Introduction to the Study of Verbal Aspect and Related Problems. Cambridge: Cambridge University Press, 1976.

Tense. Cambridge: Cambridge University Press, 1985.

Conant, T. J.
Gesenius' Hebrew Grammar: Seventeenth Edition, with Numerous Corrections and Additions by Dr. E. Rödiger. New York: D. Appleton & Co., 1856.

Cowley, A. E.
Gesenius' Hebrew Grammar. Edited and enlarged by E. Kautzsch, translated by A. E. Cowley. Second English edition. Oxford: Clarendon Press, 1910.

Dahl, Ö.
"Perfectivity in Slavic and other languages." In *Aspect Bound: A Voyage into the realm of Germanic, Slavonic, and Finno-Ugrian aspectology*, edited by C. de Groot and H. Tommola, 3–22. Dordrecht: Foris Publications and USA: Cinnaminson, 1984.

Tense and Aspect Systems. Oxford: Basil Blackwell, 1985

DeCaen, V.
"Ewald and Driver on Biblical 'Aspect': Anteriority and the Orientalist Framework," *ZAH* 9 (1996)129–51.

Doty, R. W.
"Time and Memory." In *Brain Organization and Memory*, edited by J. L. McGaugh, N. Weinberger, G. Lynch, 145–58 . New York: Oxford University Press, 1990.

Driver, S. R.
A Treatise on the Use of the Tenses in Hebrew. Third revised edition. Oxford: Clarendon Press, 1892.

Endo, Y.
The Verbal System of Classical Hebrew in the Joseph Story. An Approach from Discourse Analysis. SSN 32. The Netherlands: Van Gorcum, 1996.

Eskhult, M.
Studies in Verbal Aspect and Narrative Technique in Biblical Hebrew Prose. Uppsala: Almqvist & Wiksell, 1990.

Fenton, T. L.
"The Hebrew 'Tenses' in the Light of Ugaritic," *Proceedings of the Fifth World Congress of Jewish Studies*, vol. 4 (1969) 31–39.

Forbes, N.
Russian Grammar. Third edition. Oxford: Clarendon Press, 1964.

Friedrich, J. and Röllig, W.
Phönizisch-Punishce Grammatik. Roma: Pontificium Institutum Biblicum, 1970.

Fruchtman, M.
"A Few Notes on the Study of Biblical Narrative," *Ha-Sifrut/Literature* no.22, VI/2 (1976) 63–66 (Hebrew).

Garr, W. R.
Dialect Geography of Syria-Palestine, 1000–586 B.C.E. Philadelphia: University of Pennsylvania Press, 1985.

Gibson, J. C. L.
"Coordination by *Vav* in Biblical Hebrew." In *Words Remembered, Texts Renewed. Essays in Honor of John F. A. Sawyer,* edited by J. Davies et al. 272–79. JSOTSup 195. Sheffield: Sheffield Academic Press, 1995.

Gilliard, F. D.
"More Silent Reading in Antiquity. *Non Omne Verbum Sonabat,*" *JBL* 112 (1993) 698–94.

Gordon, A.
"The Development of the Participle in Biblical, Mishnaic, and Modern Hebrew," *Afroasiatic Linguistics* 8/3 (1982) 1–59.

Gottstein, M. H.
"Afterthought and the Syntax of Relative Clauses in Biblical Hebrew," *JBL* 68 (1949) 35–47.

Hackett, J.
The Balaam Text From Deir 'Alla. HSM 31 Chico, CA: Scholars Press, 1984.

Haywood, J. A. and Nahmad, H. M.
A New Arabic Grammar of the Written Language. Cambridge: Harvard University Press, 1962.

Hazoniel, B.
"The Double Accents of Genesis 35:22," *Beit Mikra* 42 (1996) 61–80 (Hebrew).

Heine, B., Claudi, U., Hünnemeyer, F.
Grammaticization. A Conceptual Framework. Chicago: University of Chicago Press, 1991.

Held, M.
"The YQTL-QTL (QTL-YQTL) Sequence of Identical Verbs in Biblical Hebrew and in Ugaritic." In *Studies and Essays in Honor of Abraham A. Neuman,* edited by M. Ben-Horin et al., 281–90. Leiden: Brill, 1962.

Hirtle, W. H.
Time, Aspect and the Verb. Quebec: Les Presses de L'université Laval, 1975.

Jenni, E.
"Response to P. Swiggers," *ZAH* 6 (1993) 55–59.

Johnson, B.
Hebräisches Perfekt und Imperfekt mit vorangehendem we. Lund: CWK Gleerup, 1971.

Joüon, P., Muraoka, T.
A Grammar of Biblical Hebrew. Roma: Pontificio Istituto Biblica, 1991.

Katz, J.
Semantic Theory. Evanston: Harper and Row, 1972,

Kharma, N.
A Contrastive Analysis of Verb Forms in English and Arabic. Heidelburg: Julius Groos, 1983.

Klein, G. L.
"The Prophetic Perfect," *JNSL* 16 (1990) 45–60.

Kogut, S.
Correlations Between Biblical Accentuation and Traditional Jewish Exegesis. Linguistic and Contextual Studies (Hebrew). Jerusalem: Magnes Press, 1994.

König, E.
Syntax der Hebräischen Sprache. Leipzig: J. C. Hinrichs Buchhandlung, 1897.

Krahmalkov, C.
"The *Qatal* with Future Tense Reference in Phoenician," *JSS* 31 (1986) 5–10.

Kutscher, Y.
The Language and Linguistic Background of the Isaiah Scroll (1QIsa a). Leiden: E. J. Brill, 1974.

A History of the Hebrew Language. Jerusalem: Magnes Press, 1982.

Lascarides, A.
"Knowledge, causality, and temporal representation," *Linguistics* 30 (1992) 941–73.

Licht, J.
Storytelling in the Bible. Jerusalem: Magnes Press, 1978.

Livnat, Z. and Sela, M.
"Apposition–The Third Relation?" *Leš* 59 (1995) 57–70 (Hebrew).

Loewenstamm, S. E.
From Babylon to Canaan. Jerusalem: Magnes Press, 1992.

Longacre, R.
"Discourse Peak as Zone of Turbulence." In *Beyond the Sentence, Discourse and Sentential Form*, edited by J. Wirth, 81–98. Ann Arbor: Karoma, 1985.

"*Weqatal* Forms in Biblical Hebrew Prose: A Discourse-modular Approach." In *Biblical Hebrew and Discourse Linguistics*, edited by R. D. Bergen, 50–98. USA: Summer Institute of Linguistics, 1994.

Lunt, H. G.
Fundamentals of Russian. The Hague: Mouton, 1954.

McFall, L.
The Enigma of the Hebrew Verbal System. Sheffield: Almond Press, 1982.

Mishor, M.
The Tense System in Tannaitic Hebrew (Hebrew). Ph.D. thesis submitted to the Hebrew University of Jerusalem, 1983.

Moran, W. L.
"The Hebrew Language in Its Northwest Semitic Background." In *The Bible and the Ancient Near East: Essays in Honor of William Foxwell Albright*, edited by G. E. Wright, 59–84. Garden City: Doubleday, 1961.

Müller, A.
Outlines of Hebrew Syntax. Glasgow: James Maclehose & Sons, 1882.

Muraoka, T.
Emphatic Words and Structure in Biblical Hebrew. Leiden: E. J. Brill and Jerusalem: Magnes Press, 1985.

"Linguistic Notes on the Aramaic Inscription from Tel Dan," *IEJ* 45 (1995) 19–21.

"The Tel Dan Inscriptions and Aramaic/Hebrew Tenses," *Abr-Nahrain* 33 (1995) 113–15.

Niccacci, A.
The Syntax of the Verb in Classical Hebrew Prose. JSOTSup 86. Sheffield: JSOT Press, 1990.

"Analysis of Biblical Narrative." In *Biblical and Discourse Linguistics,* edited by R. D. Bergen, 117–37. USA: Summer Institute of Linguistics, 1994.

Nordheimer, I.
A Critical Grammar of the Hebrew Language. Second edition. New York: Wiley and Putnam, 1842.

Ogunbowale, P. O.
The Essentials of the Yoruba Language. London: University of London Press, 1970.

Polak, F.
Biblical Narrative. Aspects of Art and Design (Hebrew). Jerusalem: Bialik Institute, 1994.

Provan, I. W.
"Past, present and future in Lamentations iii 52–66: the case for a precative perfect re-examined," *VT* 41 (1991) 164–75.

Qimron, E.
The Hebrew of the Dead Sea Scrolls. Atlanta: Scholars Press, 1986.

"Consecutive and Conjunctive Imperfect: The Form of the Imperfect with Waw in Biblical Hebrew," *JQR* 77 (1987) 149–61.

Rainey, A.
"The Ancient Hebrew Prefix Conjugation in the Light of Amarnah Canaanite," *HS* 27 (1986) 4–19.

"A New Grammar of Ugaritic," *Or* 56 (1988) 391–402.

Rendsberg, G. A.
"The Galilean Background of Mishnaic Hebrew." In *The Galilee in Late Antiquity,* edited by L. I. Levine, 225–40. New York and Jerusalem: The Jewish Theological Seminary of America, 1992.

Revell, E. J.
"The Conditioning of Stress Position in *Waw* Consecutive Perfect Forms in Biblical Hebrew," *HAR* 9 (1985) 277–300.

"The System of the Verb in Standard Biblical Prose," *HUCA* 60 (1989) 1–37.

Rubinstein, E.
Contemporary Hebrew and Ancient Hebrew (Hebrew). Israel: Ministry of Defense, 1980.

Sauer, W.
A Formal Semantics of Tense, Aspect, and Aktionsart. Bloomington, IN: Indiana University Linguistics Club, 1984.

Schmitz, P. C.
"A Problem of Punic Morphology: The Third Person Singular Feminine of the Suffixing Conjugation with Object Pronoun," *JSS* 40 (1995) 219–225.

Schneider, W.
Grammatik des Biblischen Hebräisch. München: Claudius Verlage, 1993. (First printed, 1974.)

Segert, S.
"Verbal Categories of Some Northwest Semitic Languages: A Didactic Approach," *Afroasiatic Linguistics* 2:5 (1975) 1–12.

A Grammar of Phoenician and Punic. München: C. H. Beck, 1976.

A Basic Grammar of the Ugaritic Language. Berkeley: University of California Press, 1984.

Sivan, D.
Ugaritic Grammar (Hebrew). Jerusalem: Bialik Institute, 1993.

Smith, C. S.
The Parameters of Aspect. Studies in Linguistics and Philosophy 43. Dordrecht: Kluwer Academic Publishers, 1991.

Smith, M. S.
The Origins and Development of the Waw Consecutive. Atlanta: Scholars Press, 1991.

"The **qatala* Form in Ugaritic Narrative Poetry." In *Pomegranates and Golden Bells: Studies in Biblical, Jewish, and Near Eastern Ritual, Law, and Literature in Honor of Jacob Milgrom*, edited by D. P. Wright, et al., 789–803. Winona Lake; Eisenbrauns, 1995.

Sternberg, M.
Expositional Modes and Temporal Ordering in Fiction. Baltimore and London: The Johns Hopkins University Press, 1978.

The Poetics of Biblical Narrative. Ideological Literature and the Drama of Reading. Bloomington, IN: Indiana University, 1985.

Talmon, S.
"The Presentation of Synchroneity and Simultaneity in Biblical Narrative,"
ScrHier 27 (1978) 9–26.

Talstra, E.
Review of Schneider, *Grammatik, BO* 35 (1979) 169–74; 39 (1982) 26–38.

Tenny, C. L.
Aspectual Rules and the Syntax-Semantics Interface. Studies in
Linguistics and Philosophy 52. Dordrecht: Kluwer Academic Publishers,
1994.

Tropper, J.
"Paläographische und linguistische Anmerkungen zur Steleninschrift aus
Dan," *UF* 26 (1994) 487–92.

Valin, R.
"The Aspects of the French Verb." An appendix in *Time, Aspect and the
Verb*, by W. H. Hirtle, 131–45. Quebec: Les Presses de L'université Laval,
1975.

van Dijk, T. A.
"Connectives in Text Grammar and Text Logic," In *Grammars and
Descriptions (Studies in Text Theory and Text Analysis)*, edited by T. A.
van Dijk and J. S. Petöfi, 11–63. Berlin: W. de Gruyter, 1977.

Washburn, D. L.
"Chomsky's Separation of Syntax and Semantics," *HS* 35 (1994) 27–46.

Waltke, B. K. and O'Connor, M.
An Introduction to Biblical Hebrew Syntax. Winona Lake, IN: Eisenbrauns,
1990

Welmers, B. F. and Welmers, W. E.
Igbo: A Learner's Manual. Los Angeles: Dept. of Linguistics, UCLA, 1968.

Welmers, W. E.
African Language Structures. Berkeley: University of California Press,
1973.

Wright, W.
A Grammar of the Arabic Language II. Third Edition. Cambridge:
Cambridge University Press, 1964.

Yeivin, I.
Introduction to the Tiberian Masorah. Translated and edited by E. J. Revell. Masoretic Studies 5. Missoula: Scholars Press, 1980.

Zakovitch, Y.
"Foreshadowing in Biblical Narrative," *Beer-Sheva* 2 (1985) 85–105 (Hebrew).

Zevit, Z.
Matres Lectionis in Ancient Hebrew Epigraphs. ASOR Monograph Series 2. USA: ASOR, 1980.

"Nondistinctive Stress, Syllabic Constraints, and Wortmetrik in Ugaritic Poetry," *UF* 15 (1983) 291–98.

"Talking Funny in Biblical Henglish and Solving a Problem of the YAQTUL Past Tense," *HS* 29 (1988) 25–33.

"Cognitive Theory and the Memorability of Biblical Poetry," *Maarav* 8 (1992) 199–212.

Author Index

Scripture Index

Genesis

2 Kings

3:3–4	27
3:4	36
4:1	46 n.15
4:38	46 n.15
4:42	46 n.15
4:30–31	27
5:1–2	46 n.15
5:24–25	30
5:26	68
6:8	46 n.15
6:32	27
7:2–3	30
7:16–17	27
8:1	46 n.15
8:10	11
8:29	29
8:29b	27, 46 n.15
9:1–13	29
9:1	27, 29, 46 n.15
9:3	55
9:14	27, 29
9:16	27
9:23–24	30
9:27	27
9:30–31	30
9:33	51 n.6
14:7	61
17:23	41
17:29–34	36
17:29–31	27
17:34	41
17:41	41
20:4	30
23:4	65
23:5	10, 65
23:8	65
23:10	65
23:12	65
23:14	65
23:15	65

Isaiah

5:13	61 n.33
6:5	61 n.33
9:1–5	61 n.33
10:28	61 n.33
11:9	61 n.33
19:7	61 n.33
29:22	71 n.1
39:1	70
43:15	61 n.33
48:41	61 n.33
55:9	57
64:4	70

Jeremiah

4:1–2	58
6:17	53 n.13
7:31	65
12:3	53 n.13, 60
17:27	58
18:4	65
19:4	65
19:5	65
20:9	53 n.13
21:14	58
24:10	58
43:12	58
44:4	61
49:26	58
51:30	61 n.33

Ezekiel

3:26	55
14:13	58
17:22	58
28:12	58
28:22	58
28:25	58
29:7	53 n.13
30:14	58
30:16	58